Ranching, Sport and Travel

Thomas Carson

Contents

RANCHING, SPORT AND TRAVEL

BY

Thomas Carson

ONE OF THE "BOYS."

INTRODUCTORY NOTE

This book is somewhat in the nature of an autobiography, covering as it does almost the whole of the Author's life. The main portion of the volume is devoted to cattle ranching in Arizona, New Mexico and Texas. The Author has also included a record of his travels abroad, which he hopes will prove to be not uninteresting; and a chapter devoted to a description of tea planting in India.

CHAPTER I
TEA PLANTING

In Cachar--Apprenticeship--Tea Planting described--Polo--In Sylhet--Pilgrims at Sacred Pool--Wild Game--Amusements--Rainfall--Return to Cachar--Scottpore--Snakes--A Haunted Tree--Hill Tribes--Selecting a Location--Return to England.

Having no inclination for the seclusion and drudgery of office work, determined to lead a country life of some kind or other, and even then having a longing desire to roam the world and see foreign countries, I had arranged to accompany a friend to the Comoro Islands, north of Madagascar; but changing my mind and accepting the better advice of friends, my start was made, not to the Comoro Islands, but to India and the tea district of Cachar. Accordingly the age of twenty-two and the year 1876 saw me on board a steamer bound for Calcutta.

Steamers were slow sailers in those days, and it was a long trip via Gibraltar, Suez, Malta, the Canal and Point de Galle; but it was all very interesting to me.

Near Point de Galle we witnessed from the steamer a remarkable sight, a desperate fight, it seemed to be a fight and not play, between a sea-serpent, which seemed to be about fifteen feet long, and a huge ray. The battle was fought on the surface of the water and even out of it, as the ray several times threw himself into the air. How it ended we could not see. Anyway we had seen the sea-serpent, though not the fabulous monster so often written about, and yet whose existence cannot be disproved. The sea-serpent's tail is flattened.

At Calcutta I visited a tea firm, who sent me up to Cachar to help at one of the gardens till a vacancy should occur. Calcutta, by the way, is or was overrun by jackals at night. They are the scavengers of the town and hunt in packs through the streets, their wolfish yelling being a little disconcerting to a stranger.

It was a long twelve days, but again a very interesting journey, in a native river boat, four rowers (or towers), to my destination. I had a servant with me, who proved a good, efficient cook and attendant. It was rather trying to the "griffin" to notice, floating in the river, corpses of natives, frequently perched upon by hungry vultures.

The tea-garden selected for me was Narainpore, successfully managed by a fellow-countryman, who proved to be a capital chap and who made my stay with him very pleasant. Narainpore was one of the oldest gardens, on teelah (hilly) land and quite healthy. There I gave what little help I could, picked up some of the lingo, and learned a good deal about the planting, growth and manufacture of tea. Neighbours were plentiful and life quite sociable. Twice a week in the cold weather we played polo, sometimes with Munipoories, a hill tribe whose national game it is, and who were then the undoubted champions. The Regent Senaputti was a keen player, and very picturesque in his costume of green velvet zouave jacket, salmon-pink silk dhotee and pink silk turban. In Munipoor even the children have their weekly polo matches. They breed ponies specially for the game, and use them for nothing else, nor would they sell their best. Still, we rode Munipoor "tats" costing us from 50 rupees to 100. They were exceedingly small, averaging not eleven hands high, but wiry, active, speedy, full of grit, and seemed to love the game. As the game was there played, seven formed a side, the field was twice as large as now and there were no goals. The ball had to be simply driven over the end line to count a score.

It may be remarked here that the great Akbar was so fond of polo, but otherwise so busy, that he played the game at night with luminous balls.

These Munipoories were a very fine race of people, much lighter of colour than their neighbouring tribes, very stately and dignified in their bearing, and thorough sportsmen. Many of their women were really handsome, and the girls, with red hibiscus blossoms stuck in their jet-black hair, and their merry, laughing faces and graceful figures, were altogether quite attractive to the Sahib Log.

But to return to tea. Our bungalow was of the usual type, consisting of cement floor, roof of crossed bamboos and two feet of sun-grass thatch, supported by immense teak posts, hard as iron and bidding defiance to the white ants. The walls were of mats. Tea-gardens usually had a surface of 300 to 1000 acres; some were on comparatively level ground, some on hilly (teelah) land. These teelahs were always carefully terraced to prevent the wash of soil and permit cultivation. The plants were spaced about three to six feet apart, according to whether they were of the Chinese, the hybrid, or the pure indigenous breed, the last being the largest, in its native state developing to the dimensions of a small tree.

I may as well here at once give a short sketch of the principal features of tea planting and manufacture, which will show what the duties of a planter are, and how various are the occupations and operations embraced. One must necessarily first have labour (coolies). These are recruited in certain districts of India, usually by sending good reliable men, already in your employ, to their home country, under a contract to pay them so much a head for every coolie they can persuade (by lies or otherwise) to come to your garden. The coolies must then bind themselves to work for you for, say, three to four years. They are paid for their work, not much it is true, but enough to support them with comfort; the men about three annas (or fourpence) a day, the women two annas (or threepence). As they get to know their work and become expert, the good men will earn as much as six annas a day, and some of the women, when plucking leaf, about the same. This is more than abundant for these people. They not only have every comfort, but they become rich, so that in a few years they are able to rest on their earnings, and work only at their convenience and when they feel like it. They are supplied with nothing, neither food nor clothing; medicine alone is free to them. The native staff of a garden

PLUCKING TEA LEAF.

consists of, say, two baboos, or book-keepers and clerks, a doctor baboo, sirdars or overseers, and chowkidars or line watchmen. A sirdar accompanies and has charge of each gang of coolies on whatever branch of work. One is also in charge of the factory or tea-house.

Plant growth ceases about the end of October. Then cold-weather work begins, including the great and important operation of pruning, which requires a large force and will occupy most of the winter. Also charcoal-burning for next season's supply; road-making, building and repairing, jungle-cutting, bridge-building, and nursery-making: that is, preparing with great care beds in which the seed will be planted early in spring. Cultivation is also, of course, carried on; it can never be overdone. In the factory, some men are busy putting together or manufacturing new tea-boxes, lining them carefully with lead, which needs close attention, as the smallest hole in the lining of a tea-chest will cause serious injury to the contents.

When spring opens and the first glorious "flush" is on the bushes, there is a readjustment of labour. Pluckers begin to gather the leaf, and as the season advances more pluckers are needed, till possibly every man, woman and child may be called on for this operation alone, it being so important that the leaf flush does not get ahead and out of control, so that the leaf would get tough and hard and less fit for manufacture; but cultivation is almost equally important, and every available labourer is kept hard at it.

What a pleasure it is to watch a good expert workman, be he carpenter, bricklayer, ploughman, blacksmith, or only an Irish navvy. In even the humblest of these callings the evidence of much training, practice or long apprenticeship is noticeable. To an amateur who has tried such work himself it will soon be apparent how crude his efforts are, how little he knows of the apparently simple operation. The navvy seems to work slowly; but he knows well, because his task is a day-long one, that his forces must be economised, that over-exertion must be avoided. This lesson was brought home to me when exasperated by the seeming laziness of the coolie cultivators, I would seize a man's hoe and fly at the work, hoe vigorously for perhaps five minutes, swear at the man for his lack of strenuousness, then retire and find myself puffing and blowing and almost in a state of collapse.

If an addition or extension is being made to the garden, the already cut jungle has to be burnt and the ground cleared in early spring, the soil broken up and staked:

that is, small sticks put in regular rows and intervals to show where the young plants are to be put. Then when the rains have properly set in the actual planting begins. This is a work that requires a lot of labour and close and careful superintendence. Imagine what it means to plant out 100 acres of ground, the plants set only three or four feet apart! The right plucking of the leaf calls for equally careful looking after. The women are paid by the amount or weight they pluck, so they are very liable to pluck carelessly and so damage the succeeding flush, or they may gather a lot of old leaf unsuited for manufacturing purposes. In short, every detail of work, even cultivation, demands close supervision and the whole attention of the planter.

When the new-plucked leaf is brought home it is spread out to wither in suitably-built sheds. (Here begins the tea-maker's responsibility.) Then it must be rolled, by hand or by machinery; fermented, and fired or dried over charcoal ovens; separated in its different classes, the younger the leaf bud the more valuable the tea. It is then packed in boxes for market, and sampled by the planter. He does this by weighing a tiny quantity of each class or grade of tea into separate cups, pouring boiling water on them, and then tasting the liquor by sipping a little into the mouth, not to be swallowed, but ejected again.

All this will give an idea of the variety of duties of a tea-planter. He has no time for shooting, polo, or visiting during the busy season. But at mid-winter the great annual Mela takes place at the station, the local seat of Government. The Mela lasts a couple of weeks, and it is a season of fun and jollity with both planters and natives. There were two or three social clubs in Silchar; horse and pony racing, polo, cricket and football filled the day, dinner and sociability the night; and what nights! The amount of liquor consumed at these meetings was almost incredible.

Nothing can look more beautiful or more gratifying to the eye of the owner than a tract of tea, pruned level as a table and topped with new fresh young leaf-shoots, four to eight inches high, in full flush, ready for the pluckers' nimble fingers.

At the end of one year I was offered and accepted the position of assistant at a Sylhet garden, called Kessoregool, the property consisting of three distinct gardens, the principal one being directly overseered by the manager, an American. He, of course, was my superior. My charge was the Lucky Cherra Gardens, some few miles away. There I spent two years, learning what I could of the business, but without the advantage of European society; in fact, the Burra Sahib and myself were almost the only whites in the district, and as he was drunk quite half the time, and we did not pull very well together, I was left to my own resources. I found amusement in various ways. There was no polo, but some of the native zemindars (landed proprietors) were always ready to get up a beat for leopards, tigers, deer and pig. Their method was simply to drive the game into a net corral and spear them to death. The Government Keddas, under Colonel Nuttal, were also not far away in hill Tipperah, and it was intensely interesting to watch operations. Close to my garden also was a sacred pool and a very beautiful waterfall. This was visited twice a year by immense numbers of natives, some from great distances, for it was a famous and renowned place of pilgrimage. It could only be approached through my garden; and as there was no wagon road, the pilgrims were always open to inspection, so to speak; and they were well worth inspection, as among them were many races, all ages, both sexes, every caste or jat; robes, turbans and cupras of every shape and colour; fakirs and wonder-workers, and beggars galore. Here, and on such an occasion only, could the sahib see face to face the harems of the wealthy natives, consisting of women who at no other time showed themselves out of doors. Being the only sahib present I had all the "fun of the fair" to myself, but always regretted the want of a companion to share it with me.

As to wild game, there were lots of jungle fowl (original stock of our familiar barn-door cocks and hens), a few pigeons, Argus pheasants, small barking deer, pigs, sambur, barrasingha, metnas, crocodiles, leopards, tigers, bears and elephants; but I had little time for shooting and it was expensive work, the jungle being so thick that riding elephants were quite necessary. If keen enough, one could sit all night on a machan in a tree near a recent "kill," on the chance of Stripes showing himself; but it never appealed to me much, that kind of sport. If a tiger was raiding the cattle I would poison the "kill" with strychnine. In this way I secured several very fine animals, getting two at one time, so successfully poisoned that their bodies actually lay on the dead bullock. One time I shot an enormous python, some eighteen feet in length, which took several men to carry home. Monkeys were plentiful and of several kinds. I was very fond of wandering amongst the high-tree jungle and quietly watching their antics. In the dense forest there is little undergrowth, so that one can move about freely and study the extraordinary forms of vegetation displayed. Ticks and leeches are to be dreaded--a perfect nuisance. If you sit down or pause for a few moments where no leeches are in sight, suddenly and quickly they will appear marching on you, or at you, at a gallop.

The popular idea of a wealth of flowers in tropical jungles is a misconception. In tree jungle no flowers are to be found, or at any rate they are not visible. But if one can by some means attain an elevation and so be able to overlook the tree-tops, he will probably be rewarded with a wonderful display, as many jungle trees are glorified with crowns of gorgeous colours. There will he also discover the honey-suckers, moths, butterflies, the beetles, and all the other insect brood which he had also vainly looked for before. The fruits are likewise borne aloft, and therefore at the proper time these tree-tops will be the haunt of the monkeys, the parrots, the bats, the toucans, and all frugivorous creation.

Of all fruits the durian is the most delicious. Such is the universal opinion of men, including A. R. Wallace, who have had the opportunity of becoming familiar with it. It is purely tropical, grows on a lofty tree, is round and nearly as large as a cocoanut. A thick and tough rind protects the delicacy contained within. When opened five cells are revealed, satiny white, containing masses of cream-coloured pulp. This pulp is the edible portion and has an indescribable flavour and consistence. You can safely eat all you want of it, and the more you eat the more you will want. To eat durian, as Mr Wallace says, is alone worth a voyage to the East. But it has one strange quality--it smells so badly as to be at first almost nauseating; some people even can never bring themselves to touch it. Once this repulsion is mastered the fruit will probably be preferred to all other foods. The natives give it honourable titles, exalt it, and even wax poetical over it.

Of course we all know the multitudinous uses of the bamboo. This grass is one of the most wonderful, beautiful and useful of Nature's gifts to uncivilized man. And yet one more use has been found for it. In the East a new industry has sprung up, viz., the making of "Panama" hats of bamboo strips or threads. In texture and pliability these hats are said to even surpass the genuine "Panamas," are absolutely impervious to rain, and can be produced at a much lower cost.

The Looshais killed pigs, and even tigers, by ingeniously setting poisoned arrows in the woods, which were released by the animals pressing on a string. One of my coolies was unfortunate enough to be shot and killed in this way.

Growing on decayed tree stumps I frequently found a saprophyte (*hymenophallus*), much larger than its English representative, indeed a monster in comparison, and possessing a vile and most odious smell, yet attractive to certain depraved insects.

I made a very fine collection of butterflies, moths and beetles, which, however, was entirely destroyed by worms or ants during its passage to England. The magnificent Atlas moth was common in Sylhet and Cachar. What an extraordinarily beautiful creature it is, sometimes so large as to cover a dinner-plate. I never was privileged to see it fly. It seemed to be always in a languid or torpid condition.

Thunderstorms occur almost daily during the wet season. By lightning I lost several people. In one case, whilst standing watching a man remove seedlings from a nursery bed, standing indeed immediately behind and close to him, there came a thrilling flash of lightning. It shook myself as well as several women who stood by. The man in front of me, who had been sitting on his haunches with a steel-ribbed umbrella over him, remained silent and still. At last I called on him to continue his work and pulled back the umbrella to see his face. He was stone dead. Examination showed a small blackish spot where the steel rib had rested and conveyed the fatal shock.

The approach of the daily rainstorm, usually about noon, was a remarkable sight. Immense fan-shaped, thunderous-looking clouds would come rolling up, billow upon billow, travelling at great speed and accompanied by terrific wind. A flash of lightning and a crashing peal of thunder and the deluge began, literally a deluge. The rainfall averaged about 180 inches in seven months. At Cherrapunji, in the Kassia Hills, within sight of my place and only about twenty miles distant, the rainfall was and is the greatest in the world, no other district approaching it in this respect, viz., averaging per annum 450 inches; greatest recorded over 900 inches; and there is a record of *one* month, July, of a fall of nearly 400 inches; yet all this precipitation takes place during the six or seven wet months, the rest of the year being absolutely dry and rainless. These measurements are recorded at the Government Observatory Station and need not be disputed. It may readily be supposed that the wet season, summer, with its high temperature and damp atmosphere, was very trying to the European, and even to the imported coolies. Imagine living for six continuous months in the hottest palm-house in Kew Gardens; yet the planter is out and about all day long; nearly always on pony back, however, an enormously thick solah toppee hat or a heavy white umbrella protecting his head. The dry, or cold season, however, was delightful.

Close to Lucky Cherra Garden was a tract of bustee land on which some Bengali cultivators grew rice and other crops. Our Company's boundary line in some way conflicted with theirs, and a dispute arose which soon developed into a series of, first, most comical mix-ups, and afterwards into desperate "lathi" fights. The land in dispute was being hurriedly ploughed by buffalo teams belonging to the Bengalis; to uphold our claim I also secured teams and put them to ploughing on the same piece of ground. This could only lead to one thing--as said before, terrific lathi fights between the teamsters. For several days I went down to see the fun, taking with me a number of the stoutest coolies on the garden. The men seemed to rather enjoy the sport, though a lick from a lathi (a formidable tough, hard and heavy cane) was far from a joke. Finally the bustee-wallahs agreed to stop operations and await legal judgment.

After eighteen months I was suddenly left in sole charge of all the Company's gardens, the Burra Sahib having finally succumbed to drink; but I was not long left in charge, being soon relieved by a more experienced man. Shortly after I was ordered to Scottpore Garden in Cachar, the manager of which, a particularly fine man and a great friend of mine, had suffered the awful death of being pierced by the very sharp end of a heavy, newly-cut bamboo, which he seems to have ridden against in the dark. He always rode at great speed, and he too, in this way, was a victim of drink. The tremendously high death-rate amongst planters was directly due to this fatal habit.

Scottpore was a new (young) garden, not teelah, but level land, having extremely rich soil. The bushes showed strong growth and there were no "vacancies"; indeed it was a model plantation. Unfortunately, it had the character of extreme unhealthiness. Of my three predecessors two had died of fever and one as before mentioned. The coolie death-rate was shocking; so bad that, during my management, a Government Commission was sent to look into the situation, and the absolute closing of the garden was anticipated. The result was that I was debarred from recruiting and importing certain coolies from certain districts in India, they being peculiarly susceptible to fever and dysentery. Almost every day at morning muster the doctor reported so and so, or so many, dead, wiped off the roll. Naturally the place suffered from lack of labour, a further draining of the force being the absconding of coolies, running off, poor devils, to healthier places, and the stealing of my people by unscrupulous planters.

On several occasions, when riding home on dark nights, have I detected white objects on the side of the road. Not a movement would be seen, not a sound or a breath heard, only an ominous, suspicious silence reigned; it meant that these were some of my people absconding, being perhaps led off by a pimp from another garden--and woe betide the pimp if caught. I would call out to them, and if they did not respond would go after them; but generally they were too scared to resist or to attempt further to escape; so I would drive them in front of me back to the garden, inspect them and take their names, try to find out who had put them up to it, etc., and dismiss them to the lines in charge of the night-watchman. You could not well punish them, though a good caning was administered sometimes to the men. Thus the plantation, instead of presenting a clean, well-cultivated appearance, had often that of an enormous hayfield; nevertheless the output and manufacture of tea was large and the quality good. All that I myself could and did take credit for was this "quality," as the prices obtained in Calcutta were the best of all the Company's gardens.

At Scottpore there was no lack of neighbours. My bungalow was on two cross-roads, a half-way house so to speak; consequently someone was continually dropping in. Frequently three or four visitors would arrive unannounced for dinner; the house was always "wide open." Whisky, brandy and beer were always on the sideboard, and in my absence the bearer or khansamah was expected, as a matter of course, to offer refreshments to all comers. The planter's code of hospitality demanded this, but it was the financial ruin of the Chota Sahib, depending solely on his modest salary.

At Scottpore I went in strong for vegetable, fruit and flower gardening, and not without success. Visitors came from a distance to view the flower-beds and eat my green peas, and I really think that I grew as fine pineapples and bananas as were produced anywhere. The pineapple of good stock and ripened on the plant is, I think, the most exquisite of all fruits. A really ripe pine contains no fibre. You cut the top off and sup the delicious mushy contents with a spoon.

In such a hot, steamy climate as we had in these tea districts, the rapidity of growth of vegetation is, of course, remarkable. Bamboos illustrate this better than other plants, their growth being so much more noticeable, that of a young shoot amounting to as much as four inches in one night. It sometimes appeared to my imagination that the weeds and grass grew one foot in a like period, especially when short of labour. The planter usually takes a pride in the well-cultivated appearance of the garden in his charge; but how can one be proud if the weeds overtop the bushes? It may be appropriate here to note that eighty-five per cent. of the twenty-four hours' growth of plants occurs between 12 p.m. and 6 a.m.; during the noon hours the apparent growth almost entirely ceases.

Garden coolies are generally Hindoos and are imported from far-off districts. The local peasantry of Bengal are mostly Mohammedans and do not work on tea-gardens, except on such jobs as cutting jungle, building, etc. They speak a somewhat different tongue, so that we had to understand Bengali as well as Hindustani. I may mention here that as Hindoos regard an egg as defiling, and Mohammedans despise an eater of pork, our love for ham and eggs alienates us from both these classes; what beasts we must be! The Hindoos and the Bengal Mussulmans are characterized by cringing servility, open insolence, or rude indifference. Contrast with this the Burmese agreeableness and affability, or the bearing of the Rajput and the Sikh. In those days the natives cringed before the Sahib Log much more than they do now. Then all had to put their umbrellas down on passing a sahib, and all had to leave the side-walk on the white man's approach; not that the law compelled them to do so, it was simply a custom enforced by their masters, in the large cities as well as in the mofussil.

We thought it advisable at all costs to keep the coolies in a proper state of subjection. Thus, when on a certain occasion a coolie of mine raised his kodalie (hoe) to strike me I had to give him a very severe thrashing. Another time a man appeared somewhat insolent in his talk to me and I unfortunately hit him a blow on the body, from the effects of which he died next day. Some of these people suffer from enlarged spleens and even a slight jar on that part of their anatomy may prove fatal.

A few more notes. Among the Sontals in Bengal the snake stone, found within the head of the Adjutant-bird, is applied to a snake bite exactly in the same way and with the same supposed results as the Texas madstone, an accretion found, it is said, in the system of a white stag. Many natives of India die from purely imaginary snake bites.

In Oude there have been many instances verified, or at least impossible of contradiction, of so-called wolf-children, infants stolen by wolves and suckled by them, that go on all fours, eat only raw meat, and, of course, speak no language.

The Nagas, a hill tribe and not very desirable neighbours, practise the refined custom of starving a dog, then supplying it with an enormous feed of rice; and when the stomach is properly distended, killing it, the half-digested mess forming the *bonne-bouche* of the tribal feast.

Snake stories are always effective. I have none to tell. My bungalow roof, the thatch, was at all times infested by snakes, some quite large. At night one frequently heard them gliding between the bamboos and grass, chasing mice, beetles, or perhaps lizards, and sometimes falling on the top of the mosquito bar, or even on the dinner-table; but these were probably harmless creatures, as most snakes are. The cobra was not common in Cachar. It may be said here that a snake's mouth opens crossways as well as vertically, and each side has the power of working independently, the teeth being re-curved backwards. Prey once in the jaws cannot escape, and the snake itself can only dispose of it in one way--downwards.

At Scottpore I employed an elephant for certain work, such as hauling heavy posts out of the jungle. Sometimes his "little Mary" would trouble him, when a dose of castor oil would be effectively administered. Unfortunately, he misbehaved, ran amok, and tried to kill his mahout, and so that hatthi (elephant) had to be disposed of. When clearing jungle for a tea-garden the workmen sometimes come on a certain species of tree, of which they are in great dread. They cannot be induced to cut it down and so the tree remains. Such a one stood opposite my bungalow, a stately, handsome monarch of the forest. It was a sacred, or rather a haunted tree, but as its shade was injurious to tea-plant growth I was determined to have it destroyed. None of my people would touch it; so I sent over to a neighbour and explained the facts to him, requesting him to send over a gang of his men to do the deed. I was to see that they had no communication with my own people. Well, his men came and were put to work with axes. The result? Two of them died that day and the rest bolted. Yet this is not more extraordinary than people dying of imaginary snake bites.

NAGAS

Shortly afterwards an incident occurred to still further strengthen the native belief that the tree was haunted. I had a very fine bull terrier which slept in the porch at night, the night-watchman also sleeping there. One time I was aroused by terrific yells from the dog, and called to the watchman to know the trouble. After apparently recovering from his fright he told me the devil had come from the tree and carried off the dog. The morning showed traces of a tiger's or leopard's pugs, and my poor terrier was of course never seen again.

The hill tribes surrounding the valley of Cachar were the Kassias, Nagas, Kookies, Munipoories and Looshais, all of very similar type, except that the Munipoories were of somewhat lighter skin, were more civilized and handsomer. The Kassias were noted for their wonderful muscular development, no doubt accounted for by their being mountaineers, their poonjes (villages) being situated on the sides of high and steep mountains. All their market products, supplies, etc., were packed up and down these hills in thoppas, a sort of baskets or chairs slung on the back by a band over the forehead. In this way even a heavy man would be carried up the steep mountain-side, and generally by a woman.

Once, in later years, whilst in Mexico, near Crizaba, I was intensely surprised to meet in the forest a string of Indios going to market and using this identical thoppa; the similar cut of the hair across the forehead, the blanket and dress, the physical features, even the peculiar grunt emitted when carrying a weight, settled for me the long-disputed question of the origin of the Aztecs. In Venezuela I saw exactly the same type in Castro's Indian troops, as also in the Indian natives of Peru.

The Kassias were fond of games, such as tossing the caber, putting the weight and throwing the hammer, apparently a tribal institution. The Kookies and Nagas were restless, warlike and troublesome, and addicted to head hunting. They periodically raided some tea-gardens to secure lead for bullets, and incidentally heads as trophies. Several planters had been thus massacred, and at outlying gardens there was always this dread and danger. On one occasion an urgent message was brought to me from such a garden, whose manager happened to be in Calcutta. His head baboo begged me to come over and take charge, if only to reassure the coolies, who had been running off into the jungle on the report of a threatened Naga raid. On going over I found the people tremendously excited, and most of them scared nearly to death. My presence seemed to allay their fright, though if the savages had come we could have done nothing, having only a few rifles in the place and the coolies totally demoralized. Luckily Mr Naga did not appear.

The Looshais were a particularly warlike race, and gardens situated near their territory were supplied by Government with stands of arms and had stockades for defence in case of attack.

The tea-planter's life was to me a very enjoyable one. There was lots of interesting work to be done, lots of sport and amusement, and lots of good fellows. The life promised to be an ideal one. For its enjoyment, however, indeed for its possibility, there is one essential--good health. Unfortunately that, during the whole period at Scottpore, was not mine; for the whole eighteen months fever had its grip on me; appetite was quite gone, and I subsisted on nothing but eggs, milk and whisky. Six months more would have done me up; but just at this time came the announcement of my father's death. For this reason and on account of my health I resigned the position and prepared to visit home, meaning to return, however, to India.

I determined before going to look out a piece of land suitable for a small plantation; and, after much consideration, decided to hunt for it in Eastern Sylhet. So bidding adieu to friends I hied me down to the selected district, secured a good man as guide (a man of intelligence and intimate knowledge of the country was essential), and hired an elephant to carry us and break a way through the jungle. In the course of our search we came to a piece of seemingly swampy ground; the high reeds which had once covered it had been eaten down and the surface of the bog trodden on till it became caked, firm and almost solid. Our path was across it, but on coming to the edge the elephant refused to proceed. On the mahout urging him he roared and protested in every way, so much so that I was somewhat alarmed and suggested to the mahout that the elephant knew better than he the danger of proceeding. Finally, however, the elephant decided to try the ground, and carefully and slowly he made his way across, his great feet at every step depressing the surface, which perceptibly waved like thin ice all around him. I was prepared and ready to jump clear at the first sign of danger, for had we broken through we should have probably all disappeared in the bog. Hatthi was as much relieved as myself on reaching terra firma. My guide told me that this land had no bottom, that under the packed surface there was twenty feet of soft, black, loamy mud. This set me thinking. I was after something of this nature. In the course of the next day we came upon a somewhat similar piece of ground, some 300 acres in extent, still covered with the original reeds and other vegetation. The soil was in places exposed and was of a rich, dark brown loamy character. Taking a long ten-foot bamboo and pressing it firmly on the ground it could be forced nearly out of sight. That was enough for me. The object sought for was found. Further tests with a spade and bamboo were made at different points; deep drainage seemed practicable, and, what was quite important, a small navigable river bounded the property. Then I hunted up a native surveyor, traced the proposed boundaries, got numbers and data, etc., to enable me to send my application to the proper quarter, which I soon afterwards did, making a money deposit in part payment to the Government. My task was completed, and I at once started for Calcutta and home.

As things turned out I never returned to the country and so had to abandon my rights, etc.; but in support of my judgment I was very much gratified to learn years afterwards that someone else had secured and developed this particular piece of land as a tea-garden, and that it had turned out to be the most valuable, much the most valuable, piece of tea land, acre for acre, in the whole country. Often and bitterly since then have I regretted not being able to return and develop and operate this ideal location. More than that, I had learned the tea-growing business, had devoted over three years to its careful study, felt myself in every way competent, and had found a life in many ways suited to my tastes. All this had to be abandoned. In India the white man lives in great luxury. He has a great staff of servants, his every whim and wish is anticipated and satisfied, his comfort watched over. To leave *this*, to go straight out to the West, the wild and woolly West, where servants were not! The very suggestion of such a thing to me on leaving India would have received no consideration whatever. It would have seemed utterly impossible, but "El Hombre propone y el Deos depone" as the Mexicans say.

During the whole four years' stay in India I was practically barred from ladies' society, nearly all the planters being unmarried men. Alas! for twenty years longer of my life this very unfortunate and demoralizing condition was to continue.

There were no railroads then to Cachar and no steamers, so I again performed the journey to Calcutta in a native boat, and there, by-the-bye, I witnessed the sight for the first time of an apparent lunatic playing a game called Golf; a game which later was to be more familiar to me, and myself to become one of the greatest lunatics of all. The run home was in no way remarkable, except for the intense anticipated pleasure of again seeing the old country.

CHAPTER II
CATTLE RANCHING IN ARIZONA

Leave for United States of America--Iowa--New Mexico--Real Estate Speculation--Gambling--Billy the Kid--Start Ranching in Arizona--Description of Country--Apache and other Indians--Fauna--Branding Cattle--Ranch Notes--Mexicans--Politics--Summer Camp--Winter Camp--Fishing and Shooting--Indian Troubles.

My health seemed to have reached a more serious condition than imagined; and so on the advice of my friends, but with much regret, I decided to henceforth cast my lot in a more bracing climate. Having no profession, and hating trade in any form, the choice was limited and confined to live stock or crop farming of one kind or another.

Accordingly, after six months at home and on complete recovery of health, I took my way to the United States of America, first to Lemars in Iowa, where was a well-known colony of Britishers, said Britishers consisting almost entirely of the gentlemen class, some with much money, some with little, none of them with much knowledge of practical business life or affairs, all of them with the idea of social superiority over the natives, which they very foolishly showed. Sport, not work, occupied their whole time and attention. Altogether it seemed that this was no place for one who had to push his fortunes. The climate, too, seemed to be far from agreeable, in summer being very hot, in winter very cold; so, with another man, I decided to go further west and south, to the sheep and cattle country of New Mexico; not that I had any knowledge of sheep or cattle, hardly knowing the one from the other; but the nature of Ranch life (Ranch with a big R) and the romance attaching to it had much to do with my determination.

Arrived in New Mexico I went to live with a sheepman--a practical sheepman from Australia--to study the industry and see how I liked it. In the neighbourhood was a cattle ranch and a lot of cowboys. I saw much of *their* life, and was so attracted by it that the sheep proposition was finally abandoned as unsuitable. Still, I was very undecided, knew little of the ways of the country and still less of the cattle business. I moved to the small town of Las Vegas, then about the western end of the Santa Fe railroad. Here I stayed six months, making acquaintances and listening to others' experiences.

Las Vegas was then a true frontier town. It was "booming," full of life and all kinds of people, money plentiful, saloons, gambling-dens and dance-halls "wide open." Real Estate was moving freely, prices advancing, speculation rife, and--I caught the infection! A few successful deals gave me courage and tempted me further. I became a real gambler. On some deals I made tremendous profits. I even owned a saloon and gambling-hall, which paid me a huge rental and gave me my drinks free! The world looked "easy."

Not content with Las Vegas, I followed the road to Albuquerque and Socorro, had some deals there and spent my evenings playing poker, faro and monte with the best and "toughest" of them. Santa Fe, the capital, was then as much a "hell" as Las Vegas.

Let me try to describe one of these gambling resorts. A long, low room, probably a saloon, with the pretentious bar in front; tables on either side of the room, and an eager group round each one, the game being roulette, faro, highball, poker, crapps or monte. The dealers, or professional gamblers, are easily distinguished. Their dress consists invariably of a well-laundered "biled" (white) shirt, huge diamond stud in front, no collar or tie, perhaps a silk handkerchief tied loosely round the neck, and an open unbuttoned waistcoat. They are necessarily cool, wide-awake, self-possessed men. All in this room are chewing tobacco and distributing the results freely on the floor. Now and then the dealers call for drinks all round, perhaps to keep the company together and encourage play. But poker, the royal game, the best of all gambling games, is generally played in a retired room, where quietness and some privacy are secured. Mere idlers and "bums" are not wanted around; perhaps the room is a little cleaner, but the floor is littered, if the game has lasted long, with dozens of already used and abandoned packs of cards. At Las Vegas the majority of the players were cowboys and cattlemen; at Socorro miners and prospectors; at Albuquerque all kinds; at Santa Fe politicians and officials and Mexicans, but Chinamen, always a few Chinamen, everywhere; and what varied types of men one rubs shoulders with! The cowpunchers, probably pretty well "loaded" (tipsy), the "prominent" lawyer, the horny-handed miner, the inscrutable "John"; the scout, or frontier man, with hair long as a woman's; the half-breed Mexican or greaser elbowing a don of pure Castilian blood; the men all "packing" guns (six-shooters), some in the pocket, some displayed openly. The dealer, of course, has his lying handy under the table; but shooting scrapes are rare. If there is any trouble it will be settled somewhere else afterwards.

But things took a turn; slackness, then actual depression in Real Estate values set in, and oh! how quickly. Like many others, I got scared and hastened to "get out." It was almost too late, not quite. On cleaning up, my financial position was just about the same as at the beginning of the campaign. It was a lesson, a valuable experience; but I admit that Real Estate speculation threw a glamour over me that still remains. It is the way to wealth for the man who knows how to go about it.

About this time two Englishmen arrived in Las Vegas, and we soon got acquainted. One could easily see that they were not tenderfeet. On the contrary, they appeared to be shrewd, practical men of affairs. They had been cattle ranching up north for some years, had a good knowledge of the business, and were "good fellows." They had come south to look out a cattle ranch and continue in the business. They wanted a little more capital, which seemed my opportunity, and the upshot was that we formed a partnership, for good or for ill, which lasted for many years (over twelve), but which was never financially successful. Considering my entire ignorance of cattle affairs, and having abounding confidence in my two partners, I agreed to leave the entire control and management in their hands.

It was about this time (1883) that I was fortunate enough to meet at Fort Sumner the then great Western celebrity, "Billy the Kid." Billy was a young cowboy who started wrong by using his gun on some trivial occasion. Like all, or at least many, young fellows of his age he wanted to appear a "bad man." One shooting scrape led to another; he became an outlaw; cattle troubles, and finally the Lincoln County War, in which he took a leading part, gave him every opportunity for his now murdering propensities, so that soon the tally of his victims amounted to some twenty-five lives. The Lincoln County New Mexico "War," in which it is believed that first to last over 200 men were killed, was purely a cattleman's war, but the most terrible and bloody that ever took place in the West. New Mexico was at that time probably the most lawless country in the world.

Only a month after my meeting Billy in Fort Sumner he was killed there, not in his "boots," but in his stockings, by Sheriff Pat Garret. He was shot practically in his bed and given no "show." His age when killed was only twenty-three years. There were afterwards many other "kids" emulous of Billy's renown, because of which, and their youthfulness, they were always the most dangerous of men.

Our senior partner, not satisfied with New Mexico, went out to Arizona for a look round, liked the prospect, and decided to locate there, so we moved out accordingly. Arizona (Arida Zona) was at this time a practically new and unoccupied territory; that is, though there were a few Mexicans, a few Mormons and a great many Indians, a few sheep and fewer cattle, it could not be called a settled country, and most of the grazing land was in a virgin state.

My partner had bought out a Mexican's rights, his cattle, water-claims, ranches, etc., located at the Cienega in Apache county, near the head-waters of the Little Colorado River. To close the deal part payment in advance had to be made; and to ensure promptness the paper was given to my care to be delivered to the seller as quickly as possible. Accordingly I travelled by train to the nearest railroad point, Holbrook, found an army ambulance about to convey the commanding officer to Camp Apache, and he was good enough to allow me to accompany him part of the way. It was a great advantage to me, as otherwise there was no conveyance, nor had I a horse or any means of getting to the ranch, about eighty miles. Judging from the colonel's armed guard and the fact of travelling at night, it occurred to me that something was wrong, and on questioning him he told me that he would not take any "chances," that the Apaches were "out" on the war-path, but that they never attacked in the dark. This lent more interest to the trip, though it was interesting enough to me simply to see the nature of the country where we had decided to make our home. We got through all right. Next morning I hired a horse and reached the ranch the same day.

As this was to be our country for many years to come, it will be well to describe its physical features, etc. Arizona, of course, is a huge territory, some 400 by 350 miles. It embraces pure unadulterated desert regions in the west; a large forest tract in the centre; the rest has a semi-arid character, short, scattering grass all over it; to the eye of a stranger a dreary and desolate region! The east central part, where we were, has a general elevation of 4000 to 6000 feet above sea-level, so that the fierce summer heat is tempered to some extent, especially after sundown. In winter there were snowstorms and severe cold, but the snow did not lie long, except in the mountains, where it reached a depth of several feet.

The Little Colorado River (Colorado Chiquito), an affluent of the Greater River, had its headquarters in the mountains, south of our ranch. It was a small stream, bright and clear, and full of speckled trout in its upper part; lower down most of the time dry; at other times a flood of red muddy water, or a succession of small, shallow pools of a boggy, quicksandy nature, that ultimately cost us many thousands of cattle. The western boundary of Arizona is the Big Colorado River. Where the Santa Fe railroad crosses it at the Needles is one of the hottest places in North America. In summer the temperature runs up to as high as 120 degrees Fahr., and I have even heard it asserted to go to 125 degrees in the shade; and I cannot doubt it, as even on our own ranch the thermometer often recorded 110 degrees; that at an elevation of 4000 feet, whereas the Needles' elevation above sea-level is only a few hundreds. At Jacobabad, India, the greatest heat recorded is 126 degrees, and at Kashan, in Persia, a month--August--averaged 127 degrees, supposed to be the hottest place on earth.

Above the Needles begins or ends the very wonderful Grand Canon, extending north for 270 miles, its depth in places being as much as 6000 feet, and that at certain points almost precipitously. The wonderful colouring of the rocks, combined with the overpowering grandeur of it, make it one of the most impressive and unique sights of the world.

Now, stop and think what that is--2000 yards! say a mile; and imagine the effect on a stranger when he first approaches it, which he will generally do without warning--nothing, absolutely nothing, to indicate the presence of this wonderful gorge till he arrives at its very brink. Its aspect is always changing according to the hour of day, the period of the year, the atmospheric conditions. The air is dry and bracing at all times; and as pure, clear and free from dust or germs as probably can be found anywhere on earth. The panorama may be described as "*wunderschoen*."

Anyone of sensibility will sit on the rock-rim for hours, possibly days, in dumb contemplation of the beauty and immensity. No one has yet, not even the most eloquent writer, been quite able to express his feelings and sentiments, though many have attempted to do so in the hotel register; some of the greatest poets and thinkers admitting in a few lines their utter inability. Our Colorado Chiquito in its lower parts has an equally romantic aspect.

Close to our ranch was another of Nature's wonders, a petrified forest, quite unique in that the exposed tree trunks are solid masses of agate, chalcedony, jasper, opal and other silicate crystals, the variety of whose colouring, with their natural brilliancy, makes a wonderfully beautiful combination. These trees are supposed to have been the Norfolk Island pine, a tree now extinct, are of large dimensions, all prostrate, lying in no particular order, and all broken up into large or smaller sections. Many carloads have been removed and shipped to Eastern factories, where the sections are sawn through and polished, and the most lovely table tops, etc., imaginable produced. One must beware of rattlesnakes when prowling about these "ruins."

To complete the physical description of Arizona territory something must be said of the pine-clad mountain range to the south of us. The bulk of this area constituted the Apache Indian Reservation. It was reserved for these Indians as a hunting-ground as well as a home. No one else was allowed to settle within its boundaries, or graze their sheep or cattle there. It was truly a hunter's paradise, being largely covered with forest trees, broken here and there by open parks and glades and meadow lands, drained by streams of clear cool water, which combining, produced a few considerable-sized rivers, "hotching" with trout, unsophisticated and so simple in their natures that it seemed a positive shame to take advantage of them. These mountains were the haunt of the elk, the big-horned sheep, black-and white-tailed deer, grizzly, cinnamon, silver tip, and brown and black bears; the porcupine, racoon and beaver; also the prong-horned antelope, though it is more of a plains country animal. But more of this some other time.

The Apache Indians (Apache is not their proper name, but Tinneh; the former was given to them by the Mexicans and signifies "enemy") were and are the most dreaded of all the redskin tribes. They always have been warlike and perhaps naturally cruel, and at the time of our arrival in the country they had about attained their most bloodthirsty and murderous character. Shocking ill-treatment by white skalawags and United States officials had changed their nature; but more about them also by-and-by.

North of us were the numerous and powerful Navajo Indians. They were not so much dreaded by us, their Reservation being further away, and they then being of a peaceful disposition, devoted to horse and sheep breeding and the manufacture of blankets.

These are the famous Navajo blankets so often seen in English homes, valued for the oddness of their patterns and colours, but used in Arizona mainly as saddle blankets. The majority of them are coarsely made and of little intrinsic value; but others, made for the chiefs or other special purposes, are finely woven, very artistic, and sell for large sums of money. Rain will not penetrate them and they make excellent bed coverings.

These Navajoes used to declare that they would never quit the war-path till a certain "Dancing Man" appeared, and that they would never be conquered till then. An American officer, named Backus, at Fort Defiance, constructed a dummy man, who danced by the pulling of wires, and showed him to the Indians. They at once accepted him as their promised visitor, and have since then never gone on the war-path. This may seem an incredible tale, but is a fact.

Also near us were the Zuni Indians, who, like the Pueblo Indians, lived in stone-built communal houses, had entirely different customs to those of the Apaches and Navajoes, and are perhaps the debased descendants of a once powerful and advanced nation. Whilst speaking of Indians, it may be said that the plains tribes, such as the Comanches, believe in the immortality of the soul and the future life. All will attain it, all will reach the Happy Hunting-Ground, unless prevented by such accidents as being scalped, which results in annihilation of the soul.

Is it not strange that though these barbarians believe in the immortality of the soul yet our materialistic Old Testament never even suggests a future life; and it seems that no Jew believes or ever was taught to believe in it.

Indian self-torture is to prove one's endurance of pain. A broad knife is passed through the pectoral muscles, and a horse-hair rope inserted, by which they must swing from a post till the flesh is torn through. Indians will never scalp a negro; it is "bad medicine." By the way, is not scalping spoken of in the Book of Maccabees as a custom of the Jews and Syrians? The tit-bits of a butchered carcass are, to the Indians, the intestines, a speciality being the liver with the contents of the gall bladder sprinkled over it! Horses, dogs, wolves and skunks are greatly valued for food.

Amongst certain tribes Hiawatha was a Messiah of divine origin, but born on earth. He appeared long ago as a teacher and prophet, taught them picture-writing, healing, etc.; gave them the corn plant and pipe; he was an ascetic; told them of the Isles of the Blessed and promised to come again. In Mexico Quetzalcohuatl was a similar divine visitor, prophet and teacher.

But to return to our own immediate affairs. At a reasonable price we bought out another cattleman, his ranches, cattle and saddle horses. As required by law, we also adopted and recorded a cattle brand. Our first business was to brand our now considerable herd, which entailed an immense amount of very hard work. This in later years would have been no very great undertaking, but at that time "squeezers" and branding "chutes" were not known. Our corrals were primitive and not suited for the work, and our cattle extraordinarily wild and not accustomed to control of any kind. Indeed, the men we had bought out had sold to us for the simple reason that they could not properly handle them. The four-legged beasties had got beyond their control, and many of them had almost become wild animals. These cattle, too, had very little of the "improved" character in them. Well-bred bulls had never been introduced.

Some of the bulls we found had almost reached their allotted span--crusty old fellows indeed and scarred in many a battle; "moss-heads" we called them, and the term was well applied, for their hoary old heads gave the idea of their being covered with moss.

Most of the cattle had never been in a corral in their lives, and some of the older steers were absolute "outlaws," magnificent creatures, ten to twelve years of age, with immense spreading horns, sleek and glossy sides, and quite unmanageable. They could not be got into a herd, or if got in, would very soon walk out again. Eventually some had to be shot on the range like any wild animal, simply to get rid of them; but they at least afforded us many a long and wild gallop.

There was one great steer in particular, reckoned to be ten or twelve years old, quite a celebrity in fact on account of his unmanageableness, his independence and boldness, which we had frequently seen and tried to secure, but hitherto without success. He had a chum, another outlaw, and they grazed in a particular part of the range far from the haunts of their kin and of man. Three of us undertook to make one more effort to secure him. At the headquarters ranch we had gathered a herd of cattle and we proposed to try and run the steer in that direction, where the other boys would be on the lookout and would head him into the round-up. Two of us were to go out and find the steer and start him homewards; I myself undertook to wait about half-way, and when they came in sight to take up the running and relieve them. They found him all right about twenty miles out, turned him and started him. No difficulty so far. He ran with the ease of a horse, and he was still going as he willed, without having the idea of being coerced. Meantime I had been taking it easy, lolling on the ground, my horse beside me with bridle down. Suddenly the sound of hoof-beats and a succession of yells warned me to "prepare to receive cavalry." Through a cleft in a hill I could see the quarry coming at a mad gallop directly for me, the two men pounding along behind. I had just time and no more to tighten girth and get into the saddle when he was on me, and my horse being a bit drowsy it needed sharp digging of the spurs to get out of the way. I forget how many miles the boys said they had already run him, but it was a prodigious distance and we were still eight miles from the ranch. The steer was getting hot, it began to suspect something, and to feel the pressure. As he came down on me he looked like a mountain, his eyes were bright, he was blowing a bit, and looked particularly nasty. When in such a condition it does not do to overpress, as, if you do, the chances are the steer will wheel round, challenge you and get on the fight. Much circumspection is needed. He will certainly charge you if you get too near, and on a tired horse he would have the advantage. So you must e'en halt and wait--not get down, that would be fatal--wait five minutes it may be, ten minutes, or a quarter of an hour, till the gentleman cools off a bit. Then you start him off again, not so much driving him now, he won't be driven, but guiding his course towards the herd. In this case we succeeded beautifully, though at the end he had to be raced once more. And so he was finally headed into the round-up; but dear me, he only entered it from curiosity. No round-up for him indeed! no corral and no going to market! He entered the herd, took a look round, a sniff and a smell, and was off again out at the other side as if the devil was after him, and indeed he wasn't far wrong. The chase was abandoned and his majesty doomed later on to a rifle bullet wherever found.

Our principal and indeed only corral at that time was of solid stone walls, a "blind" corral, and most difficult to get any kind of cattle into. While pushing them in, each man had his "rope" down ready to at once drop it over the horns of any animal attempting to break back. Thus half our force would sometimes be seen tying down these truants, which were left lying on the ground to cool their tempers till we had time to attend to them; and it is a fact that some of these individuals, especially females, died where they lay, apparently of broken hearts or shame at their subjection. They showed no sign of injury by rough usage, only their damnable tempers, rage and chagrin were responsible for their deaths.

Inside the corral everything, of course, had to be roped and thrown to be branded. It was rough and even dangerous work, and individual animals, again generally cows, would sometimes make desperate charges, and even assist an unfortunate "puncher" in scaling the walls. In after years we built proper corrals, and in the course of time, by frequent and regular handling, the cattle became more docile and better-mannered. For one thing, they were certainly easily gathered. When we wanted to round them up we had only to ride out ten or twenty miles, swing round and "holler," when all the cattle within sight or hearing would at once start on the run for the ranch. These were not yet domesticated cattle in that they always wanted to run and never to walk. Indeed, once started it was difficult to hold them back. This was not very conducive to the accumulation of tallow on their generally very bare bones.

I well remember the first bunch of steers sold off the ranch, which were driven to Fort Wingate, to make beef for the soldiers. About two hundred head of steers, from six to twelve years of age, all black, brown, brindle or yellow, ne'er a red one amongst them; magnificently horned, in fair flesh, perfect health and spirits; such steers you could not "give away" to-day; but we got sixty dollars apiece for them and were well rid of them; and how they walked! The ponies could hardly keep up with them; and what cowman does not know the pleasure of driving fast walking beef cattle? Ne'er a "drag" amongst them! You had only to "point" them and let them "hit the trail"; but a stampede at night was all the more a terrific affair, though even in such a case if they got away they would keep together, and when you found one you found them all. Such a bunch of magnificent, wild, proud-looking steer creatures will never be seen again, in America at least, because you cannot get them now of such an age, nor of such primitive colours; colours that, I believe, the best-bred cattle would in course of long years and many generations' neglect revert to.

The method adopted when an obstreperous steer made repeated attempts to leave the herd was to send a bullet through his horn, which gave him something to think about and shake his head over. No doubt it hurt him terribly, but it generally was an effective check to his waywardness. And when some old hoary-headed bull wanted to "gang his ain gait" a piece of cactus tossed on to his back, whence it was difficult to shake off, would give him also something to think about.

Another small herd we some time later disposed of were equally good travellers, and indeed were driven from the ranch in one day to Camp Apache, another military post, a distance of over 40 miles. In this case the trail was through forest country where there was no "holding" ground, so they had to be pushed through.

Our herd increased and throve fairly well for a number of years till other "outfits" began to throw cattle into the country, and sheepmen began to dispute our right to certain grazing lands. We did not quite realize it at the time, but it was the beginning of the end. We had gone into a practically virgin country, controlled an immense area, and the stock throve accordingly. But others were jealous of our success, threw in their cattle as already said, and their sheep, and ultimately we swamped one another. The grass was eaten down, over-grazed, droughts came, prices broke, and so the end. From 500 our annual calf brand mounted to 4000; halted there, and gradually dropped back to the original tally. Our cattle, from poverty, bogged in the river, or perished from hunger. This was all due to the barbarous grazing system under which we worked, the United States refusing to sell or lease land for grazing purposes; consequently, except at the end of a gun, one had no control over his range. Cattle versus sheep wars resulted, stealing became rampant and success impossible.

Among other sales made was that of some 1500 steers, of all ages, which we drove right up to the heart of Colorado and disposed of at good prices. This drive was marked by a serious stampede, on a dark night in rough country, by which two of the boys got injured, though happily not seriously. Then another time we made an experimental shipment of 500 old steers to California, to be grazed and fattened on alfalfa. They were got through all right and put in an alfalfa field, and I remained in charge of them. Our cattle were not accustomed to wire fences, or being penned up in a small enclosure, and of course had never seen alfalfa; so for a week or more they did nothing but walk round the fence, trampling the belly-high lucerne to the ground. Gradually, however, they got to eating it, and in six weeks began to pick up. Briefly stated, this adventure was a financial failure. Like the cattle I had been myself an entire stranger to the wonderful alfalfa plant, and I never tired marvelling at its exuberance of growth and its capacity for supporting animal life. The heat in San Joachin Valley in high summer is almost overpowering, and vegetable growth under irrigation quite phenomenal. Alfalfa was cut some six or seven times in the season; each time a heavy crop. After taking cattle out of one pasture, then grazed bare, it was only three weeks till the plant was in full growth again, in full flower, two feet high and ready for the reception of more live stock. The variety of animal life subsisting on alfalfa was extraordinary. All kinds of domestic stock throve on it and liked it. In our field, besides cattle, were geese, ducks, turkeys, rabbits and hares in thousands, doves and quails in flocks, and gophers innumerable; frogs, toads, rats and mice; while bees, wasps, butterflies and moths, and myriads of other insects were simply pushing one another out of the way. It was a wonderful study.

In Utah much difficulty was found in growing clover. This was accounted for by the fact that there were no old maids in that polygamous country. Old maids naturally were not allowed! And there being none, there were of course no cats to kill the mice that eat the bumble-bees' nests; thus, no bumble-bees to fertilize it, therefore no clover. Old maids have found their function.

Figs could not be grown successfully in California till the Smyrna wasp had been imported to fertilize the flower.

And while talking of bees: on the Mississippi River bee-keepers are in the habit of drifting their broods on rafts up the river, following the advance of spring and thus securing fresh fields and pastures new of the young spring blossoms; which is somewhat similar to the Chinaman's habit of carrying his ducks (he does love ducks), thousands of them, on rafts and boats up and down the broad Yangtse to wherever the richest grazing and grub-infested beds may be found.

I should not forget to say that care must be used in putting cattle on alfalfa. At some seasons it is more dangerous than at others. A number of these steers "bloated," and I had to stick them with a knife promptly to save their lives. A new experience to me, but I soon "caught on."

But something must be said about our little county town, San Juan, county seat of Apache County in which we were located. St Johns consisted of one general store, three or four saloons, a drug store, a newspaper office, court-house, jail, etc. A small settlement of Mormons, who confined themselves to farming on the narrow river bottom, and an equal number of Mexicans, an idle and mischievous riffraff, though one or two of them had considerable herds of sheep, and others were county officials. County affairs were dreadfully mismanaged and county funds misused. For our own protection we had to take part in politics, form an Opposition, and after a long struggle, in which my partners did noble service, we carried an election, put in our own officials, secured control of the county newspaper, and had things as we wanted them. But it was a bitter fight, and the old robber gang, who had run the county for years, were desperate in their resentment. Unfortunately, this resentment was basely and maliciously shown by an attempt, successful but happily not fatal, to poison one of my partners. He had a long and grim fight with death, but his indomitable will pulled him through. I myself, though I had little to do with politics, had a narrow escape from a somewhat similar fate. Living at that time, in winter, at what was called the Meadows Camp, I usually had a quarter of beef hung in the porch. Frost kept it sweet and sound for a long period, and every day it was my practice to cut off a steak for consumption. There were two cats, fortunately, and a slice was often thrown to them. One morning I first gave them their portion, then cut my own. In a few minutes the unfortunate animals were in the throes of strychnine poisoning and died in short order. It was a shock to me and a warning.

The Mexicans continued for some time to be mean and threatening. Bush-whacking at night was attempted, and they even threatened an attack on our head-quarters ranch; but we were a pretty strong outfit, had our own sheriff, and by-and-by a number of good friends.

In our district rough country and timber prevented the cattle drifting very much. In winter they naturally sought the lower range; in summer they went to the mountains. Headquarters was about half-way between. It was finally arranged that I should take charge of the lower winter camp during winter and the mountain camp during summer. My partners mostly remained at headquarters. In summer time, from April to the end of October, this arrangement suited me very well indeed; in fact, it was made at my own suggestion; and the life, though a solitary one for long periods, suited me to the ground and I enjoyed it immensely. Practically I lived alone, which was also my own wish, as it was disagreeable to have anyone coming into my one-roomed cottage, turning things over and making a mess. I did my own cooking, becoming almost an expert, and have ever since continued to enjoy doing so. Of course I could have had one of the boys to live with me; but no matter what good fellows cowboys generally are, their being in very close companionship is not agreeable, some of their habits being beastly. Thus it came about that my life was a very solitary one, as it had been in India, and as it afterwards continued to be in New Mexico and Texas. Few visitors came to my camp in summer or winter. Now and then I was gladdened by a visit of one or other of my partners, one of whom, however, cared nothing for fishing or shooting, and the other was much of the time entirely absent from the country. During our short periodical round-ups of course I attended the "work" with the rest; but to spend one whole month, as I did once, without not only not conversing with, but absolutely not seeing a human being, is an experience that has probably come to very few men indeed. However, as said before, life in the White Mountains of Arizona was very enjoyable. Peaks ran up to 10,000 feet; and the elevation of my camp was about 8000 feet. Round about were extensive open parks and meadows, delightfully clear creeks and streams; grass a foot high, vast stretches of pine timber, deep and rocky canons, etc., etc.

When we first shoved our cattle up there the whole country was a virgin one, no settlements or houses, no roads of any kind, except one or two Indian hunting trails, no cattle, sheep or horses. There were, as already stated, elk, mountain sheep, antelope, deer, bears, panthers, porcupines, coons, any amount of wild turkey, spruce grouse, green pigeons, quail, etc., etc. There were virgin rivers of considerable size, swarming with trout, many of which it was my luck to first explore and cast a fly into. Most of this lovely country, as said before, was part of the Apache Indian Reservation, on which no one was allowed to trespass; but the boundary line was ill-defined and it was difficult to keep our cattle out of the forbidden territory. Indeed, we did not try to do so.

The Indian settlement was at Fort Apache, some thirty miles from my camp. These people, having such an evil reputation, are worthy of a few more notes. Such tales of cruelty and savagery were told of them as to be almost incredible. They were the terror of Arizona and New Mexico, yet they were not entirely to blame. Government ill-treatment of Cochise, the great chief of the Chiricaua Apaches, had set the whole tribe on the war-path for ten years. A military company, called the Tombstone Toughs, was organized in Southern Arizona to wipe them out, but accomplished nothing. Finally, America's greatest Indian fighter, General Crook, was sent to campaign in Arizona in 1885. The celebrated chiefs, Geronimo and Natchez, broke out again and killed some twenty-nine white people in New Mexico and thirty-six in Arizona before Crook pushed them into the Sierra Madre Mountains in Sonora, where at last Geronimo surrendered. Victorio was an equally celebrated Apache war-chief and was out about the same time. Fortunately these last raids were always made on the south side of the Reservation. We were happily on the north side, and though we had frequent scares they never gave us serious trouble. So here were my duties and my pleasures.

The saddle horses when not in use were in my care. The cattle also, of course, needed looking after. I was in the saddle all day. Frequently it would be my delight to take a pack-horse and go off for a week or two into the wildest parts of the Reservation, camp, and fish and shoot everything that came along, but the shooting was chiefly for the pot. Young wild turkeys are a delicacy unrivalled, and I became so expert in knowing their haunts that I could at any time go out and get a supply. One of my ponies was trained to turkey hunting. He seemed to take a delight in it. As soon as we sighted a flock, off he would go and take me up to shooting range, then stop and let me get two barrels in, and off again after them if more were needed. Turkeys run at a great rate and will not rise unless you press them.

Big game shooting never appealed to me much. My last bear, through lack of cartridges to finish him, went off with a broken back, dragging himself some miles to where I found him again next morning. It so disgusted me as to put me off wishing to kill for killing's sake ever afterwards. A wounded deer or antelope, or a young motherless fawn, is a most pitiable sight.

There was, and perhaps still is, no better bear country in America than the Blue River district on the border of Arizona and New Mexico. On these shooting and fishing trips I was nearly always alone, and many times experienced ridiculous scares. Camping perhaps in a deep canon, a rapid stream rushing by, the wind blowing through the tall pines, the horses tethered to tree stumps, a menagerie-like

ROPING A GRIZZLY. (By C. M. Russell.)

smell of bears frequently quite apparent, your bed on Mother Earth without tent or covering, if your sleep be not very sound you will conjure up all sorts of amazing things. Perhaps the horses take fright and run on their ropes.

You get up to soothe them and find them in a lather of sweat and scared to a tremble. What they saw, or, like men, imagined they saw or heard in the black darkness, you cannot tell. Still you are in an Indian country and perhaps thirty miles from anywhere. Many a night I swore I should pack up and go home at daylight, but when daylight came and all again seemed serene and beautiful--how beautiful!--all fear would be forgotten; I would cook my trout or fry the breast of a young turkey, and with hot fresh bread and bacon grease, and strong coffee.--Why, packing up was unthought of!

One of my nearest neighbours was an old frontiers-man and Government scout. He had married an Apache squaw, been adopted into the tribe (White Mountain Apaches) and possessed some influence. He liked trout-fishing, so once or twice I accompanied him with his party, said party consisting of his wife and all her relatives--indeed most of the tribe. The young bucks scouted and cut "sign" for us (another branch of the Apaches being then on the war-path), the women washed clothes, did the cooking, cleaned and smoked the fish, etc. These Indians were rationed with beef by the Government, while they killed no doubt quite a number of our cattle, and even devoured eagerly any decomposed carcass found on the range; but they preferred the flesh of horses, mules and donkeys, detesting pork and fish.

In these mountains in summer a serious pest was a green-headed fly, which worried the cattle so much that about noon hour they would all congregate in a very close herd out in the open places for self-protection. No difficulty then in rounding up; even antelope and deer would mix with them. When off on a fishing and hunting trip it was my custom to set fire to a dead tree trunk, in the smoke of which my horses would stand for hours at a time, even scorching their fetlocks.

In these mountains, too, was a place generally called the "Boneyard," its history being that some cattleman, stranger to the country, turned his herd loose there and tried to hold them during the winter. A heavy snowfall of several feet snowed the cattle in so that they could not be got out or anything be done with them. The whole herd was lost and next spring nothing but a field of bones was visible.

At another time and place a lot of antelope were caught in deep snow and frozen to death. A more remarkable case was that of a bunch of horses which became snowed in, the snow being so deep they could not break a way out. The owner with great difficulty managed to rescue them, when it was found they had actually chawed each other's tails and manes off.

Indian dogs have a great antipathy to white men, likewise our own dogs towards Indians, which our horses also share in. Horses also have a dread of bears. Once when riding a fine and high-strung horse a bear suddenly appeared in front. Knowing that my mount, as soon as he smelt the bear, would become uncontrollable, I quickly shot the bear from the saddle, and immediately the scared horse bolted.

To preserve trout I sometimes kippered them and hung them up to dry. Quickly the wasps would attack them, and, if not prevented, would in a short space of time leave absolutely nothing but a skeleton hanging to the string. It was later demonstrated that cattle, too, thought them a delicacy, no doubt for the salt or sugar ingredients. Snakes also have a weakness for fish, and I have seen them approach my trout when thrown on the river bank and drag them off for their own consumption.

While fishing or shooting one must always be on the careful lookout for rattlesnakes. In the rough canons and river banks the biggest rattlers are found, and you may jump, tumble or scramble on the back of one and run great chance of being bitten. On the open prairie, where smaller rattlers are very plentiful, they always give you warning with their unique, unmistakable rattle. Once, on stooping down to tear up by the roots a dangerous poison weed, in grasping the plant my hand also grasped a rattlesnake. I dropped it quick enough to escape injury, but the cold sweat fairly broke out all over me. The bite is always painful, but not always necessarily fatal.

"Rustlers" is the common name given to cattle or horse thieves. Arizona had her full share of them. That territory was the last resort of outlaws from other and more civilized states. Many of our own "hands" were such men. Few of them dare use their own proper names; having committed desperate crimes in other states, such as Texas, they could not return there. Strange to say, the worst of these "bad" men often made the best of ranch hands. Cowboys as a class, that is, the genuine cowboys of days gone by, were a splendid lot of fellows, smart, intelligent, self-reliant and resourceful, also hard and willing workers. If they liked you, they would stay with you in any kind of trouble and be thoroughly loyal. No such merry place on earth as the cow camp, where humour, wit and repartee abounded. The fact of every man being armed, and in these far-off days probably a deadly shot, tended to keep down rowdyism and quarrelling. If serious trouble did come up, it was settled then and there quickly and decisively, wrongly or rightly. Let me instance a case.

In round-up camp one day a few hot words were suddenly heard, guns began to play, result--one man killed outright and two wounded. The case of one of the wounded boys was rather peculiar. His wound was in the thigh and amputation was necessary. Being a general favourite, we, myself and partners, took turns nursing him, dressing his wounds and cheering him up as well as we could. He rapidly recovered, put on flesh and was in high spirits, and, as the doctor said, quite out of danger; but one day this big strong young fellow took it into his foolish head that he was going to die. Nothing would persuade him to the contrary, and so die he did, and that without any waste of time. In preparing a body for burial it is the custom, a burial rite indeed, not to wrap the corpse in a shroud, but to dress it in a complete ordinary costume, a brand-new suit of black clothes, white shirt, socks, etc., etc.--whether boots or not I forget, but rather think so--dress him probably better than the poor fellow was ever dressed before, and in this manner he was laid in the ground. The man who started the shooting was named "Windy M'Gee," already an outlaw, but then cook for our mess wagon. Shortly afterwards he killed a prominent lawyer in our little town, or at least we suspected him strongly, though another man suffered for the crime; but such incidents as these were too common to attract world-wide attention.

On another occasion one of our men got shot in the thigh, by whom or how I do not now remember, but he was a different sort of man from the boy just mentioned. We knew him to be quite a brave, nervy man in action, having been in one of our fighting scrapes with rustlers; but as a patient he showed a most cowardly disposition, developing a ferocious temper, rejecting medical advice, cursing everybody who came around, so that he lay for months at our charge, until we really got to wish that he would carry out his threat of self-destruction. He did not, but he was crippled for life and did not leave a friend behind.

Then, too, the cowboy, in matter of accoutrements, was a very splendid fel

A SHOOTING SCRAPE. (By C. M. Russell.)

low indeed. His saddle was gaily decorated with masses of silver, in the shape of buttons, buckles and trimmings, etc. Likewise his bridle and bit; his spurs were works of loving art from the hands of the village metal-worker, and likewise heavily plated with silver. The rowels were huge but blunt-pointed, and had little metal bells attached. His boots cost him near a month's pay, always made to careful order, with enormously high and narrow heels, as high as any fashionable woman's; his feet were generally extremely small, because of his having lived in the saddle from early boyhood up. He wore a heavy woollen shirt, with a gorgeous and costly silk handkerchief tied loosely round his neck. His head-covering was a very large grey felt hat, a "genuine Stetson," which cost him from five to twenty dollars, never less. To keep the big hat in place a thong or cord is tied around and below the back of the head instead of under the chin, experience having proved it to be much more effective in that position. His six-shooter had plates of silver on the handle, and his scabbard was covered with silver buttons. It should be said that a saddle, such as we all used, cost from forty to sixty dollars, and weighed generally about forty pounds, not counting saddle blankets. Sometimes the saddle had only one "cinch" or girth, generally two, one of which reached well back under the flank. Such heavy saddles were necessary for heavy work, roping big cattle, etc. The stirrups were then generally made of wood, very big and broad in sole and very heavy, sometimes covered with tapaderos, huge leather caps to save the feet from thorns in heavy brush, and protect them from cold in severe weather.

To protect our legs we wore over the trousers heavy leather chaparejos, sometimes of bear or buffalo hide. Let it be noted that a genuine cowpuncher never rolls his shirt sleeves up, as depicted in romancing novels. Indeed he either protects his wrists with leather wristlets, or wears long gauntlet gloves. Mounted on his favourite horse, his was a gay cavalier figure, and at the "Baillie" he felt himself to be irresistible to the shy and often very pretty Mexican senoritas. There you have a pretty faithful picture of the cowboy of twenty-five years ago.

It remains to say something of the "shooting irons." In the days of which I write there was no restriction to the bearing of arms. Every man carried a six-shooter. We, and most of our outfit, habitually carried a carbine or rifle as well as the smaller weapon. The carbine was carried in a scabbard, slung from the horn, under the stirrup flap, and so under the leg. This method kept the weapon steady and left both

ONE OF OUR MEN. (To show the hand of six-shooter.)

arms free. By raising the leg it was easily got at, and it interfered in no way with the use of the lariat (La Riata). The hang of the six-shooter required more particular consideration; when needed it would be needed *badly*, and therefore must be easily drawn, with no possible chance of a hitch. The butt of a revolver must point forwards and not backwards, as shown in the accompanying illustration, a portrait of one of our men as he habitually appeared at work. We ourselves did not go the length of wearing three belts of cartridges and two six-shooters; but two belts were needed, one for the rifle and the other for the smaller weapon. Some of the boys were always getting into scrapes and seemed to enjoy protracted fights with the Mexicans. There must be no flap to the scabbard, and the point must be tied by a leather thong around the thigh to keep it in correct position; and of course it was hung on the right side and low down on the hip, so as to be easily got at. Only when riding fast was a small loop and silver button passed through the trigger guard to prevent the gun from jolting out and being lost. The chambers were always kept full and the weapons themselves in perfect working order. Very "bad" men tied back or removed the trigger altogether, cocking and releasing the hammer with the thumb, or "fanning" it with the left hand. This permitted of very rapid firing, so that the "aar would be plumb full of lead."

As an instance of quick shooting, two of our neighbours had threatened to kill each other at sight: and we were all naturally interested in the results. When the meeting did take place, quite unpremeditated, no doubt, each man saw the other about the same instant, but one of them was just a little the quicker, and put a bullet through his enemy's heart. It was a mortal wound of course; but before the unlucky man fell he was also able to "get his work in," and both fell dead at the same instant. This was no duel. The first to fire had the advantage, but the "dead" man was too quick for him, and he did not escape. If I remember right, a good riddance.

There was one other way of "packing a gun." It was called the Arizona way. Legal gentlemen, some gamblers, and others who for various reasons wished to appear unarmed, simply put the pistol in the coat side pocket, and in use fired from that position through the pocket. It was not often so used, but I have known cases of it. In this way it was difficult to know whether a man was "heeled" (armed) or not. Of course our usual weapon, the long Colt 45 deg. six-shooter could not be so used, being too cumbrous.

1883 IN ARIZONA. AUTHOR AND PARTY.

CHAPTER III
CACTUS RANCHING IN ARIZONA--*continued*

The Cowboy--Accoutrements and Weapons--Desert Plants--Politics and   Perjury--Mavericks--Mormons--Bog Riding.

The "rustling" of cattle was very common in Arizona in these days. By "rustling" is not meant the petty burning out of a brand, or stealing of calves or odd beef cattle. It was carried on on the grand scale. Bands of rustlers operated together in large bodies. Between our range and the old Mexican border extended the Apache Reservation, a very large tract of exceedingly rough country, without roads of any description, the only signs of human presence being an occasional Indian trail and abandoned wickyups. Beyond the Reservation lay certain mining towns and camps, such as Clifton, Camp Thomas, Tombstone, and others; and then the Mexican frontier.

The rustlers' business was to steal cattle, butcher them in the mountains, and sell the beef to the mining towns; or drive them over into Old Mexico for disposal, and then again drive Mexican cattle or horses back into Arizona. Some of these gangs were very powerful and terrorized the whole country, so much so that decent citizens were afraid "to give them away."

Our cattle ranged well into the mountains, and up to a certain period we had no occasion to think that any "dirty" work was going on; but at last we "tumbled" to the fact that a gang was operating on our range. Word was brought us that a bunch of some 200 cattle had been "pulled" (Scotch, lifted). I was off the ranch at the time, but one of my partners at once started on the trail with three of the men. After some days very hard riding they caught up on the thieves at early dawn, in fact when still too dark to see very well. Shooting began at once. None of our men were hurt. Two of the enemy were badly wounded, but managed in the darkness to scramble off into the rocks, or were carried off by their companions. Our party captured their saddle horses and camp outfit, but did not feel themselves strong enough to continue the chase in such a country. The cattle were found close to the camp, but so footsore that it was impossible to move them homewards. They then returned to the ranch, and we at once organized a strong force of some seventeen men, well mounted and abundantly supplied with ammunition, etc. Again taking the trail we met the cattle on their way home, and gave them a push for a mile or so; and thinking them safe enough we prepared to continue south.

On arriving at the scene of last week's fight we noticed that the big pine trees under which the rustlers camped had gun-rests notched in the sides of them, not newly made, but showing that they had been cut a long while ago, probably in anticipation of just what had happened.

That day in camp, a horseman, the most innocent-looking of individuals, appeared, took dinner with us, and gave some plausible reason for his presence in that out-of-the-way place. It is strictly against cowboy etiquette to question a guest as to his personality, his movements or his occupation. We, however, felt very suspicious, especially as after he had gone we stumbled on to a coffee-pot and frying-pan, still warm, which had evidently been thrown into the bushes in great haste. In fact, this confirmed our suspicions that our visitor was one of the gang, and we thereafter stood careful guard round our horses every night. The cattle we decided to leave alone to take their chances of getting home, thinking the rustlers would not have the "gall", in face of our near presence, to again try to get off with them; but they did! These cattle never reached the ranch. Had they been left alone their wonderful homing instinct would certainly have got them there just as quick as they could travel. However, we did not realize the fact of the second raid till on our return no sign of these cattle could be found. So we continued south, passing through the roughest country I ever set eyes on, the vegetation in some places being of the most extraordinary nature, cacti of all kinds forming so thick a jungle that one could hardly dismount. Such enormous and freakish-looking growths of this class of plant few can have ever looked on before. The prickly pear "nopal" was the most common, and bore delicious, juicy and refreshing fruit. Indeed, being out of water and short of "chuck," we were glad to accept Nature's offering, but at a dreadful cost, for in a little while our mouths and tongues were a mass of tiny, almost invisible spines, which the most careful manipulation of the fruit could not prevent. But the most astonishing of these growths was the pitahaya (correct name saguarro), or gigantic columnar cactus, growing to a height of thirty to fifty feet, bearing the fruit on their crowns; a favourite fruit of the Pima Indians, though by what means they pluck it it would be interesting to know. Besides an infinite variety of others of the cactus family, there were yuccas, agaves and larreas; the fouquiera and koberlinia, long and thorny leafless rods; artemisias and the algarrobbas or mesquite bean-trees, another principal food of the Indians and valuable for cattle and horses. The yucca when in full bloom, its gigantic panicles bearing a profusion of large white bells, is one of Nature's most enchanting sights. Besides all these were massive biznagas, cholas, bear-grass or palmilla, and the mescal, supplying the principal vegetable food of the Apaches. Never in Texas, Arizona, or even Old Mexico, have I seen such a combination of varieties of such plants growing in such profusion and perfection; but being no botanist, and quite incompetent to give a proper appreciation of these wonders, we will return to the trail.

At one place, hidden in a canon, we ran on to a stone-built and fortified butchering establishment, but without sign of life around. Continuing, we finally came to Clifton, the copper-mining town, then perhaps the "hardest" town in Arizona. The townspeople appeared pleased to see us. Martial law was prevailing, and they seemed to think we were a posse deputized to assist in restoring order. Anyway, the sheriff informed us that nearly thirty men had left the town that day for their camp, a fortified position some ten or fifteen miles away. They were all rustlers, and somehow or other had heard of our coming. Mr Sheriff was also kind enough to advise us that we were not nearly strong enough to tackle them; so adopting his advice, after securing supplies, we rode off, and by travelling all night and working round avoided the enemy's "position." Next day we unexpectedly ran on to a large bunch of our own cattle quietly grazing on the hillside. We rounded them up, but our brands were so completely burned out and effaced that, when we put them in the corral at Camp Thomas and claimed ownership, the sheriff refused to acknowledge it, and we had to draw his attention to a small jaw brand lately adopted by us but unnoticed by the thieves, and therefore not "monkeyed" with. This was proof enough, and so our long and tedious trip was to some extent compensated for. The particular rustlers we were after we could hear nothing of, except one man, who was lying wounded at a certain establishment, but who was carefully removed before we got to the place.

On returning home there were only two possible passes through the mountains. It was lucky we took the one, as the other, we afterwards learned, had been put into a state of defence and manned by the outlaws, who in such a place could have shot us all down without danger to themselves.

This short narrative will give some sort of idea of the state of the country at that period. Thereafter it became necessary that the cattle in the mountains should be more carefully guarded and looked after, and the duty fell to me to "cut sign." By "cutting sign" is meant, in this instance, the riding round and outside of all our cattle, pushing back any that had strayed too far, and carefully looking out for fresh sign (footprints) of cattle or horses leading beyond our range limits. Such sign was always suspicious, and the trail must be followed till the stock was found and accounted for. If horse tracks accompanied the cattle it would be a dead sure proof that something was wrong. I continued this work for a long time, but nothing suspicious occurred. At last, one day when searching the open country with my field-glasses, I was gratified and at the same time alarmed to see three or four men driving a considerable herd of cattle in the direction, and on exactly the same trail as before taken by the rustlers. Convinced that all was not right, and quite realizing that there was the prospect of serious trouble for myself, I lit out for them, keeping as well under cover as possible, till, on mounting a small tree-covered knoll, I found myself directly overlooking their camp. There were the cattle, from four to five hundred, and there the men, preparing their mid-day meal, four of them in all, and all strangers to me. It was necessary at all costs to know who they were, so I was obliged to disclose myself by going into their camp. The number of saddle horses they had with them led me to think that they were not real professional cattle thieves. Had they been indeed rustlers it would have been a risky thing to do, as they would have had to dispose of me in some way or other. By my horse brand they at once knew what "outfit" I belonged to. Their brands, however, were strange to me. They asked me to eat, of course; and I soon found out that their party was headed by one Pete----, whose reputation I had often heard of as being of the worst. He said he had been grazing these cattle in some outlying park, and was now taking them home to his ranches somewhere in New Mexico. That was all right; but since he had passed through part of our range it was necessary to inspect the herd. This he resisted by every means he could think of, asserting that they were a "clean" bunch, with no "strays," and that he was in a great hurry to push on. I insisted, however, on riding through them, when, not much to my surprise, I found about twenty large unbranded calves, apparently without their "mammies." On asking Pete for an explanation: "Oh," he said, "the mammies were shore in the herd" and he "warn't no cow thief," but on my persisting he finally exclaimed, "Well, take your damned *caves* and let's get on," or some such words; so I started in and cut out nearly twenty big unbranded calves, which certainly did not have their mothers with them; which, therefore, were clearly not his property; were probably ours, but whether they were or not did not matter to me. Pete and his men pulled out home, but I caught and branded over half of these calves before turning them loose, and it is probable we got the rest of them at the next round-up. When a man is single-handed and has to make his fire up as well as catch and tie down the calves he has his hands pretty full. In this case I used only one fire and so had to drag the calves up close to it; every bit of tie rope in my pocket, thongs cut off the saddle, even my pocket-handkerchief, were all brought into service; as at one time there were as many as four calves tied down at once. I had only the one little branding-iron, a thin bent iron rod, generally carried tied to the saddle alongside the carbine. The branding-iron must be, if not quite red-hot, very nearly so. Then the calf has to be ear-marked and altered.

When the mothers are near by the bellowing of the young ones as the hot iron burns into the hide makes them wild with fear and anxiety, and the motherly instinct to charge is strained to the utmost, though they seldom dare to do it. The calves themselves, if big and stout enough, will often charge you on being released, and perhaps knock you over with a painfully hard punch.

This was merely an adventure which lent some excitement and interest to the regular work. Happily no more serious raid on our cattle occurred in that direction, but one never knew when a little "pulling" might take place and so had to be constantly on the alert.

About this time certain ill-disposed individuals tried "to get their work in on us" by asserting land frauds on our part. They tried every possible way to give us "dirt," that is, to put us to trouble and expense, and even send us to the pen if they could. They succeeded in having me indicted for perjury by the Grand Jury at Prescott, the then capital of Arizona. It cost us some money, but no incriminating evidence was forthcoming and the trial was a farce. The trial jury consisted of miners, cattlemen, saloon-keepers and others, and by mixing freely with them, standing drinks, etc., we managed to "correct" any bad feeling there might have been against us. Certainly these jurymen might have made trouble for me, but they did not. This notwithstanding that my friend, a special land agent sent out from Washington and principal witness against me, swore that I had assaulted him at a lonely place (and I well remember the occasion), and that he felt his life in such danger that he had to travel with a guard, etc. This came from politics.

Having described summer life and occupations, and before going to winter camp, something must be said about our headquarters ranch, situated some twenty miles off. Here were the grain-house, the hay stacks, wagon sheds, corrals, the kitchen, general messroom, the bunk house and private rooms for ourselves. There was a constant succession of visitors. Nearly every day some stranger or neighbour "happened" in for a meal. Everyone was welcome, or at least got free board and lodging and horse feed. There being a paid cook made things different.

But it was hot down here in summer-time, hot and dry and hardly attractive. The lower part of the range was much of it sandy country. With the temperature at 110 deg. in the shade the sand would get so hot as to be almost painful to walk on, certainly disagreeable to sit on. And when one wanted to rest the only shade you could find would be in the shadow of your horse, which at noon meant your sitting right under him; and your saddle, on remounting, would be so hot as to be really very uncomfortable. Between round-ups there was not much work to do. Before round-up a general shoeing of the horses had to be gone through. I shod my own, except in cases of young ones undergoing the operation for the first time, when assistance was needed. Except poker every night we had few amusements. It was almost a daily programme, however, to get our carbines and six-shooters out and practise at targets, firing away box after box of ammunition. No wonder we were pretty expert shots, but indeed it needs much practice to become so.

It should be said that amongst our visitors there were, no doubt, many angels whom we entertained unawares; but also, and no doubt of this, many blackguards and desperadoes, "toughs" and horse-thieves.

An old English sailor, who had farmed a little in the mountains, was on one occasion left alone at our headquarters to take charge of it during our absence on the work. Two men came along and demanded something which the old man would not give and they deliberately shot him dead. We caught the miscreants, but could not convict them, their plea being self-defence. They really should have been hung without trial.

Lynchings of cattle and horse thieves and other criminals were not then uncommon. I have twice come on corpses swinging in the wind, hung from trees or telegraph posts. But the most distressing sight witnessed was in Denver's fair city when a man, still alive, was dragged to death all through the streets by a rope round his neck, followed by a howling mob!

By the way, a strange couple once surprised me at my mountain camp, viz., two individuals dressed much alike, both wearing the hair in a long pigtail, both dressed in leather "chaps," high-heeled boots, woollen shirts, big felt hats, rifles and six-shooters, and both as "hard"-looking as they ever make them. One was a man, the other a woman! They volunteered to me nothing of their business, but I watched the horses a little closer. And I may as well here give another little incident that occurred in my summer camp.

A United States cavalry officer appeared one day at my door and demanded that I at once move the cattle off the Reservation. This was a sudden and rather big order. I told him that I was alone and could not possibly do it at once, or for several days. "Oh," he said, he "would help me," he having some forty nigger troopers with him. "All right," I said, and took the men along with me, got back behind the cattle, spread these novel cowboys out and began to drive, when such a shouting and shooting of guns took place as never was heard before in these parts. We drove the cattle, really only a thousand head or so, back to the supposed Reservation border, quite unmarked and vague, and so left them, only to wander back again at their leisure to where they had been. The officer made all kinds of threats that he would turn the Indians loose on them, but nothing more was then done.

At my winter camp, some thirty-five miles below headquarters, there was a good three-roomed frame house, a corral, etc., and the Little Colorado River flowed past near by. It was to these lower parts of the range that most of our cattle drifted in winter time. Two or three other large cattle-ranches marched with us there.

A small Mormon settlement was not far off. These Mormons were a most venturesome people and daring settlers. Certainly they are the most successful colonists and a very happy people. Living in close community, having little or no money and very little live stock to tempt Providence (rustlers), theirs is a peaceable, though possibly dull, existence. They had frequent dances, but we Gentiles were not admitted to them.

In winter one lives better than in the hot weather, table supplies being more varied. In summer, excepting during the round-ups, we never had butcher meat, and in my camp butter, eggs and milk were not known; but in winter I always had lots of good beef, potatoes, butter and some eggs from the Mormons, but still no milk. This was varied, too, by wild duck, teal and snipe shot along the river bottom.

Talking of snipe, it is very wonderful how a wounded bird will carefully dress and apply down and feathers to the injury, and even apply splints and ligatures to a broken limb.

My principal duties at this season consisted in riding the range on the lookout for unbranded calves, many calves always being missed on the round-up. This was really rather good sport. Such calves are generally big, strong, fat, and run like jackrabbits, and it takes a fast and keen pony to catch them. Occasionally you would be lucky enough to find a maverick, a calf or a yearling so old as to have left its mother and be still running loose without a brand and therefore without an owner. It was particular satisfaction to get one's rope, and therefore one's brand, on to such a rover, though it might really not be the progeny of your own cattle at all. It was no easy job either for one man alone to catch and brand such a big and wild creature, especially if among the brush and cedar trees. A certain stimulant to your work was the fact that you were not the only one out on a maverick hunt. There were others, such as your neighbours, or even independent gentlemen, expert with the rope and branding-iron, who never bought a cow critter in their lives, but started their herds by thus stealing all the calves they could lay hands on. A small crooked iron rod, an iron ring, or even an old horseshoe, did duty as branding-iron on these occasions. The ring was favoured by the latter class of men, as it could be carried in the pocket and not excite suspicion. Of course we branded, marked and altered these calves wherever we found them. "Hair branding" was a method resorted to by dishonest cowboys; by burning the hair alone, and not the hide, they would apparently brand the calf with its rightful owner's brand; but later, when the calf had grown bigger and left its mother, they would slap on their own brand with comparative safety. One had to be constantly on the lookout for such tricks.

The Mexicans, too, were fond of butchering a beef now and then, so they too required watching; but my busiest time came with early spring, when the cattle were in a poor and weak condition. The river-bed, too, was then in its boggiest state. Cattle went in to drink, stuck, and could not get out again, and thus some seasons we lost enormous numbers of them. Therefore I "rode bog" every day up and down the river. When I found an animal in the mud I had to rope it by the horns or feet and drag it by main force to solid ground. A stout, well-trained horse was needed. It was hard, dirty work and exasperating, as many of those you pulled out never got up again, and if they did would invariably charge you. No special tackle was used; you remain in the saddle, wrap the rope round the horn and dig the spurs in. Of course, on your own beat, you dragged out all you could, no matter of what brand; but when, as often happened, you failed to get them out, and they belonged to someone else, you were not allowed to shoot them; so that there the poor creatures lay for days, and perhaps even weeks, dying a lingering, but I am glad to think and believe not a painful, death. What an awful death for a reasoning, conscious man. Dumb animals, like cattle, happily seem to anticipate and hope for nothing one way or another. Once I found a mare in the river in such a position under a steep bank that nothing could be done for her. Her young colt was on the bank waiting and wondering. Very regretfully I had to leave them and carefully avoided passing that way for some days to come till the tragedy had terminated. The Little Colorado River, and afterwards the Pecos River in New Mexico, I have often seen so thick with dead and dying cattle that a man might walk up and down the river on the bodies of these unfortunate creatures. The stench would become horrible, till the spring flood came to sweep the carcasses to the sea or covered them up with deposit.

Quicksand is much more holding than mere river mud. If only the tip of the tail or one single foot of the animal is covered by the stuff, then even two stout horses will not pull it out. The Pecos River is particularly dangerous on account of its quicksandy nature, and it was my custom, when having to cross the mess wagon, to send across the ramuda of two or three hundred saddle horses to tramp the river-bed solid beforehand. On one occasion when crossing quite a small stream my two driving ponies went down to their hocks, so that I had to cut the traces and belabour them hard to get them out. Had they not got out at once they never would have done so. My ambulance remained in the river-bed all night and till a Mexican with a bull-team luckily came along next day.

At the Meadows, my winter camp, I had to fill a contract of two or three fat steers for the town butcher every week. With a man to help me we had to go far afield and scour the range to get suitable animals, the best and fattest beeves being always the furthest out. After corralling, which might mean a tremendous amount of hard galloping and repeated failures, the most difficult part of the job was the actual killing, which I accomplished by shooting them with a six-shooter, not a carbine. Only when a big steer has its head down to charge can you plant a bullet in exactly the right spot, a very small one, too, on the forehead, when he will drop like a stone. It was very pretty practice, but risky, as to get them to charge you must be afoot and inside the corral. The butcher was rather astonished when I first accomplished this trick, but it saved time and a lot of trouble. Such were my winter duties.

Sometimes neighbours would look in, and the weekly mail and home papers helped to pass the time. I read a great deal, and so the solitariness of the position was not so trying as one might suppose. Indeed, books were more to me than the neighbours' society.

"Incidents" occurred, of course, but I will only mention one. In winter I only kept up two saddle horses, picked ponies, favourites and almost friends. They were fed with grain night and morning, and, to save hay, were allowed to graze out at night. They regularly returned at early morning for their feed, so I never had to go after them. One morning, however, they did not appear. It was quite unaccountable to me and very awkward, as it left me afoot and unable to do anything. Not till about 10 a.m. did they come galloping in, greatly excited, their tails in the air, puffing and snorting. It did not look quite right. Someone had been chasing them. At noon, while preparing early dinner, a man, a stranger, rode up to the house, and of course was invited to eat. He was very reticent, in fact would hardly speak at all, and gave no hint as to who he was or anything about himself. While eating there was suddenly a rapid succession of rifle-shots heard outside. We both rushed to the door and saw a man riding for life straight to the house, with half a dozen others shooting at him from horseback. He was not touched, only his horse being killed at the door. The new-comer and my strange guest at once showed that they were very intimate indeed, so that I quickly and easily put two and two together. The following party in the meantime had stopped and spread out, taking positions behind the low hills and completely commanding the house. Only their big hats showed and I could not make out whether they were Mexicans or white men. My two guests would tell me nothing, except to assert that they knew nothing of their followers, or why they began shooting. Realizing that these two had me at their mercy, that they could make me do chores for them, fetch water, cook, feed and attend to the horses till nightfall, when with my own two fresh mounts they might possibly make a bolt for it, I got a bit anxious, and determined to find out who the larger party were. So walking out and waving my hat I caught their attention and, on advancing further, one of the party came out and met me. They were neighbouring cattlemen, and explained that the two men in my house were rustlers, and they were determined to take them dead or alive. They asked me to join their party as they were going to "shoot up" the house if necessary. To this I would not consent and went back. After a deal of talk and persuasion the two men finally agreed to give me their guns, preliminary to meeting two of the other party, who were also asked to approach unarmed. They met, much to my relief, and when, somehow or other, the two men allowed themselves to be surrounded by the rest they saw the game was up and surrendered. Then the funny thing happened and the one reason for the telling of this story. They all came down to the house, had dinner together, chatted and cracked jokes, and not a word was said about the immediate trouble. They were all "punchers," had worked together, knew each other's affairs, etc., etc. The one party was about to send the other to the penitentiary, or perhaps the gallows; but you would have thought it was only a pleasant gathering of long-separated friends. The two rustlers were lodged in the county jail, quickly broke out, and soon afterwards died in their "boots," one at the hands of the sheriff.

For tracking jail-breakers Indians, Navajoes or Apaches were sometimes employed, and the marvellous skill they showed was simply astonishing and inexplicable; all done by reading the "sign" left by the escaping party, but "sign" often quite unnoticeable to the white man. Indeed, an Indian would follow a trail by sign much as a hound will do by scent.

Talking of scent, the homing instinct of horses and cattle is very wonderful and mysterious; but it is not generally known that a horse has also great power of scent. A horse will follow its mate (nearly all horses have their chums) many miles merely by sense of smell, as my long experience of them has amply proved to me. On one occasion I for some reason displaced the near horse of my driving team and hitched up another. After driving a distance of fifteen miles and returning homewards on the same road, soon in the distance could be seen said near horse busy with nose on the ground picking up the trail, and so absorbed in it that even when we got up quite close he did not notice us. When he did recognize his chum and companion his evident satisfaction was affecting.

CHAPTER IV
ODDS AND ENDS

Scent and Instinct--Mules--Roping Contests--Antelopes--The Skunk--Garnets--Leave Arizona.

This shall be a sketchy chapter of odds and ends, but more or less interesting according to the individual reader. The horse's intelligence is nothing compared to that of the mule, and as riding animal in rough country a mule should always be used. In Mexico, Central American States and the Andes mules are alone used; and what splendid, even handsome, reliable creatures they are on roads, or rather trails, such as it would be hazardous to take horses over. I once saw the unusual sight of two big strong mules (our ammunition pack animals) roll together down a very steep hillside. Happily neither mules nor loads were at all damaged, but it was a steepish hill, as on our returning and trying to climb it we had to dismount and hang on to the horses' tails. Another good point about mules is that they will not founder themselves. Put an open sack of grain before a hungry mule and he will eat what he wants, but never in excess, whereas a horse would gorge and founder himself at once.

As said before, the homing instinct of horses and cattle is very remarkable. I have known horses "shipped" by a railway train in closed cars to a distance of over 400 miles, some of which on being turned loose found their way back to their old range. Cattle, too, may be driven a hundred or two hundred miles through the roughest country, without roads or trails of any kind, and even after being held there for several weeks will at once start home and take exactly the same route as that they were driven over, even though there be no "sign" of any kind to guide them and certainly no scent.

WOUND UP. (Horse tangled in rope.) (By C. M. Russell.)

On my shooting and fishing trips I rode one horse and packed another. The packed horse, on going out, had to be led, of course, unless indeed he was my saddle-horse's chum. But on going home, after even a couple of weeks' absence, I simply turned the pack-horse loose, hit him a lick with the rope, and off he would go with the utmost confidence as to the route, and follow the trail we had come out on, each time a different trail be it remembered, with ridiculous exactitude; yet there was no visible track or sign of any kind. Indeed, I would often find myself puzzled as to our whereabouts and feel quite confident we were at fault, when suddenly some familiar tree or landmark, noticed on going out, would be recognized.

Parts of our Arizona range were covered with great beds of broken malpais rock, really black lava, hard as iron, with edges sharp and jagged. Over such ground we would gallop at full speed and with little hesitation, trusting absolutely to our locally-bred ponies to see us through. English horses could never have done it, and probably no old-country horseman would have taken the chances. We got bad falls now and then, but very seldom indeed considering conditions.

The bits used then were murderous contrivances, being of the kind called spade or ring bits. By means of them a horse could be thrown on his haunches with slight effort, even his jaw may be broken. Luckily the bit is little used by the cowboy. His horse knows its painful character, and so obeys the slightest raising of the rider's hand. It should also be remarked that the cow-pony is guided, not by pulling either the right or left rein, but by the rider carrying his bridle hand over to the *left* if he wants to go to the left, and vice versa. There is no pulling on the mouth. The pony does not understand that; it is the slight pressure of the right rein on the *right* side of the neck that turns him to the *left*.

The reata in those days was nearly always made of plaited raw hide, and often made by the boys themselves, though a good reata required a long time to complete and peculiar skill in the making of it. Quirts (quadras) and horse hobbles were also made of raw hide.

As everyone knows, the horn of the saddle is used in America to hold roped cattle with. In South America a ring fixed to the surcingle is used; while in Guatemala and Costa Rica the reata is tied to the end of the horse's tail!

It is a very pretty sight to see a skilled roper (the best are often Mexicans) at work in a corral or in a herd; or better still, when after a wild steer on the prairie.

But roping is hardly ever used nowadays, one reason of the "passing" of the old-time cowboy. We used to have great annual roping competitions in New Mexico and Texas, when handsome prizes were given to the men who would rope and tie down a big steer in quickest time. I once or twice went in myself to these competitions and was lucky enough to do fairly well, being mounted on a thoroughly trained roping horse; but it is a chancy affair, as often the best man may unluckily get a lazy sort of steer to operate on, and it is much more difficult to throw down such an animal than a wild, active, fast-galloping one; for this reason, that on getting the rope over his horns you must roll him over, or rather *flop* him over, on to his back by a sudden and skilful action of your horse on the rope. If properly thrown, or flopped hard enough, the steer will lie dazed or stunned for about half a minute. During that short period, and only during that short period, you must slip off your horse, run up to the steer and quickly tie his front and hind feet together, so tightly and in such a way that he cannot get up. Then you throw up your hands or your hat, and your time is taken. While you are out of your saddle your horse will, if well trained, himself hold the steer down by carefully adjusting the strain on the rope which still connects the animal's horns with the horn on the saddle.

I may here tell a wonderful story of a "buck" nigger who sometimes attended these gatherings. He was himself a cowboy, and indeed worked in my neighbourhood and so I knew him well. He was a big, strong, husky negro, with a neck and shoulders like a bull's. You cannot hurt a nigger any way. Well, this man's unique performance was to ride after a steer, the bigger and wilder the better, and on getting up to him to jump off his horse, seize the steer by a horn and the muzzle, then stoop down and grip the animal's upper lip with his teeth, turn his hands loose, and so by means of his powerful jaws and neck alone throw down and topple the steer over. The negro took many chances, and often the huge steer would fall on him in such a way as would have broken the neck or ribs of any ordinary white man. In this case also the steer must be an active one and going at a good pace, otherwise he could not be thrown properly.

Stock-whips were never allowed. Useful as they may be at times, still the men are liable to ill-treat the cattle, and we got on quite well without them. Dogs, too, of course, were never used and never allowed on the range. They so nearly resemble the wolf that their presence always disturbs the cattle.

This deprivation of canine society, as it may be imagined, was keenly felt by us all, perhaps more especially by myself. Had I only then had the companionship of certain former doggy friends life would have been much better worth living. As a protection at night too, when out on long journeys across the country, during the hunting and fishing trips, or even at the permanent camps, the presence of a faithful watch-dog would probably have saved me from many a restless night.

The Navajo Indian's method of hunting antelope was to strew cedar branches or other brush in the form of a very long wing to a corral, lying loose and flat on the ground. The antelope on being driven against it will never cross an obstruction of such a nature, though it only be a foot high, but will continue to run along it and so be finally driven into the corral.

And antelope are such inquisitive animals! On the Staked Plains of New Mexico the Mexicans approach them by dressing themselves up in any ridiculous sort of fashion, so as least to resemble a human being. In this way they would not approach the antelope, but the antelope would approach them, curious to find out the nature of such an unusual monstrosity. Antelope, there, were still very plentiful, and even in my own little pasture there was a band of some 300 head. Only at certain times of the year did they bunch up together; at other times they, though still present, were hardly noticeable.

I would like to make note of the curious misnaming of wild animals in North America. Thus, the antelope or pronghorn is not a true antelope, the buffalo is not a buffalo, the Rocky Mountain goat is not a goat, and the elk is not an elk. By the same token the well-known "American aloe," or century plant, is not an aloe, but an agave.

While in Arizona I used to carry in a saddle pocket a small sketch-book and pencil, and on finding one of the beautiful wild flowers the Rocky Mountains are so famous for, that is, a new kind, I would at once get down and take a sketch of it, with notes as to colour, etc. The boys were at first a bit surprised, and no doubt wondered how easily an apparent idiot could amuse himself. I was considerably surprised myself once when busy sketching on the banks of a brawling stream in the mountains. A sudden grunt as of a bear at my elbow nearly scared me into the river. On turning round, there was an armed Apache brave standing close behind me; but he was only one of a hunting party. What sentiment that grunt expressed

I never learnt.

It is remarkable how a range or tract of country that has been overstocked or over-grazed will rapidly produce an entirely new flora, of a class repugnant to the palate of cattle and horses. In this way our mountain range in particular, when in course of a very few years it became eaten out, quickly decked itself in a gorgeous robe of brilliant blossoms; weeds we called them, and weeds no doubt they were, as our cattle refused to touch them. Certain nutritious plants, natives of the soil, such as the mescal, quite common when we first entered the country, were so completely killed out by the cattle that later not a single plant of the kind could be found.

Amongst the fauna of Arizona was, of course, the ubiquitous prairie dog; and as a corollary, so to speak, the little prairie owl (*Athene cunicularis*), which inhabits deserted dog burrows and is the same bird as occupies the Biscacha burrows in Argentina. Rattlesnakes, so common around dog-towns, enter the burrows to secure the young marmots. Another animal frequently seen was the chaparral-cock or road-runner, really the earth cuckoo (*Geococcyx Mexicanus*), called paisano or pheasant, or Correcamino, by the Mexicans. It is a curious creature, with a very long tail, and runs at a tremendous rate, seldom taking to flight. Report says that it will build round a sleeping rattlesnake an impervious ring of cactus spines. Its feathers are greatly valued by Indians as being "good medicine," and being as efficacious as the horseshoe is with us.

A still more curious animal, not often seen, was the well-named Gila monster or Escorpion (*Heloderma suspectum*), the only existing animal that fills the description of the Basilisk or Cockatrice of mediaeval times; not the *Basilicus Americanus*, which is an innocent herbivorous lizard. This Gila monster is a comparatively small, but very hideous creature, in appearance like a lizard, very sluggish in its movements, and rightly owning the worst of reputations. Horned toads, also hideous in appearance, and tarantulas (*Mygales*), very large centipedes and scorpions, were common, and lived on, or rather were killed because of their reputation, but they seldom did anyone harm.

But the most highly appreciated, that is the most feared and detested, of wild creatures was the common skunk, found everywhere, mostly a night wanderer and a hibernator. He is a most fearless animal, having such abundant and well-reasoned confidence in his mounted battery, charged with such noxious gases as might well receive the attention of our projectile experts. The first time I ever saw one he came into my mountain hut. Knowing only that he was "varmint" I endeavoured to kill him quickly with a spade. Alas! the spade fell just a moment too late and henceforth that hut was uninhabitable for a month. The only way to get one out of the house is to pour buckets of cold water on it. That keeps the tail down (unlike a horse, which cannot kick when his tail is up); but when his tail goes up, then look out! The skunk is also more dreaded by the cowboy and the frontiers-man than the rattlesnake. It is their belief that a bite from this creature will always convey hydrophobia. Being a night prowler it frequents cow camps, and often crawls over the beds spread on the ground, and it certainly has a habit of biting any exposed part of the human body. When it does so, the bitten man at once starts off to Texas, where at certain places one can hire the use of a madstone. The madstone is popularly supposed to be an accretion found somewhere in the system of a white stag. It is of a porous nature, and if applied to a fresh wound will extract and absorb the poison serum. Texans swear that it "sticks" only if there be poison present--does not stick otherwise. A fanciful suggestion! And yet, no doubt, the skunk does sometimes convey hydrophobia through its bite. I have myself often had the pleasant experience of feeling and knowing that a skunk was crawling over my carefully-covered-up body. But enough of this very objectionable creature.

In Texas some of the boys used to carry in their pockets a piece of "rattlesnake root," which when scraped and swallowed after a bite was held to be an antidote, though otherwise a virulent poison.

In this placid land of ours, so free of pests, mosquitoes, fleas and leeches, we are also free of the true skunk; but we do have, as perhaps you are aware, a small creature armed and protected in much the same way. This is the bombardier-beetle, common in certain other countries, but also found in England, which if chased will discharge from its stern a puff of bluish-white smoke, accompanied by a slight detonation. It can fire many shots from its stern chasers. It is said that a highly volatile liquid is secreted by glands, which when it meets the air passes into vapour so suddenly as to produce the explosion.

The Mexicans of the United States deserve more than a passing notice. Many of them have Indian blood and are called Greasers, but the majority are of fairly pure Spanish descent. Contact with the Americans has made them vicious and treacher

WATERING A HERD.

ous. They have been robbed of their lands, their cattle and their horses, bullied and ill-treated in every possible way. But even now many of them retain their character, almost universal amongst their compatriots in Old Mexico, for hospitality, unaffected kindness, good breeding and politeness. A Mexican village in autumn is picturesque with crimson "rastras" of Chile pepper hung on the walls of the adobe houses. To the Mexicans we owe, or rather through them to the Aztecs, the delightfully tasty and delicious enchiladas and tamales.

Among native animals should not be forgotten the common jacket-rabbit (hare). She affords capital coursing, and someone has said runs faster than an ice boat, or a note maturing at a bank, so she must indeed be speedy. It is interesting to recall that puss in Shakespeare's time was *he* and not *she*. Among our feathered friends the humming-bird was not uncommon. These lovely but so tiny little morsels are migrants. Indeed one of the family, and one of the tiniest and most beautiful, is known to summer in Alaska and winter in Central America; thus accomplishing a flight twice a year of over two thousand miles.

An interesting little note too may be made of the fact that the garnets of Arizona are principally found on ant-heaps, being brought to the surface by the ants and thrown aside as obstructions only fit for the waste-basket. But they are very beautiful gems and are regularly collected by the Indians.

There was little or no gold mining in our part of the territory; but there were current many tales of fabulously rich lost Claims, lost because of the miners having been massacred by the Indians or other causes. In likely places I have myself used the pan with the usual enthusiasm, but luckily never with much success.

The practice of that very curious custom, the "couvade," seems to be still in force among some of the Arizona Indian tribes, among whom so many other mysterious rites and customs prevail.

The loco-weed (yerba-loco) was common in our country and ruined many of our horses, but more about it hereafter.

After ten years, a long period of this life in Arizona, an offer came to me which, my partners consenting, was gladly accepted, viz., to take charge of and operate certain cattle-ranches in New Mexico in the interests of a Scottish Land and Mortgage Company. Things had not been going well with us and the future held out no prospects of improvement. Also I had been loyal to my agreement not to take or seek any share in the management of affairs, and the natural desire came to me to assume the responsibility and position of a boss. But dear me! had I foreseen the nature of the work before me, and the troubles in store, my enthusiasm would not have been quite so great.

CHAPTER V
RANCHING IN NEW MEXICO

The Scottish Company--My Difficulties and Dangers--Mustang Hunting--Round-up described--Shipping Cattle--Railroad Accidents--Close out Scotch Company's Interests.

Bidding good-bye to Arizona I travelled to Las Vegas, New Mexico, now quite an important place. Calling on Mr L----, the manager of the Mortgage Company, and the Company's lawyers, the position of affairs was thus stated to me. The Company had loaned a large sum of money to a cattleman named M----, who owned a large ranch with valuable water-claims and a very fine though small herd of cattle. M---- had paid no interest for several years and attempted to repudiate the loan, so the Company decided to foreclose and take possession. Well, that seemed all right; so after getting power of attorney papers, etc., from the Company, I started down to the ranch, some eighty miles and near Fort Sumner, and introduced myself to M----, who at once refused to turn over the property to me or to anyone else, and sent me back to Las Vegas in a somewhat puzzled state of mind. Recounting my experience to Mr L---- and the lawyers, after a long confab they decided that I should go down again and *take* possession. They refused me the services of a sheriff or a deputy to serve the papers and represent the law. No, I was to take possession in any way my wits might suggest; they merely proposing that everything I did I should put on paper and make affidavit to and send up to them. By this time I had learned that M---- was very much stirred up about it, was quite determined to give nothing up, and that really he was a dangerous man who, if pushed to extremities, might do something desperate. The lawyers told me there was another, a right, usual and legal way of taking possession, but for private reasons they did not wish to proceed in that way; and so I finally agreed to go down again and do what I could.

Buying some horses and hiring a Mexican vaquero to show me the country, and especially to be a witness to whatever took place, we pulled out for Fort Sumner. The spring round-up was about to begin, and near by I found M----'s "outfit" wagon, "cavayad" of horses, his full force of "hands" and the foreman H----. After dining with them I pulled out my papers to show H---- who I was and told him I had come there to take possession of M----- 's saddle horses, the whole "ramuda" in fact of nearly a hundred head. Oh, no! he had no instructions to give them up; he did not know anything of the matter and he certainly would not let me touch them! I said I had come to carry out my orders and meant to do so; and mounting, rode out to gather up the grazing ponies. At once they came after me, not believing that anyone would dare do such a thing in their presence, and began to jostle me, with more evil intentions in their eyes. Desisting at once, and before they had gone too far, I told them that that was all I wanted, said good-bye in as friendly a way as possible, and went before a Justice of the Peace and made affidavit of having attempted to take possession of the horses till resisted by force, in fact, that physical violence had been used against me. This was sent to Las Vegas, and in due course the lawyers advised me that it was satisfactory and recommended me to adopt similar methods when attempting to get possession of the ranches, cattle, stock horses, etc.

This was a funny position to be in! M----was a popular man; the other cattlemen would certainly side with him and resent such novel and apparently high-handed proceedings. Myself was an entire stranger in the whole of that huge country, devoted solely to cattle interests, and of course did not have a friend nor did expect to have any. In fact M---- 's appellation of me as that "damned Scotsman" became disagreeably familiar. The round-up was then a long way off down the river, some 100 miles, working up towards Fort Sumner; so I decided to visit the ranches. We rode out to one where was a house (unoccupied) and a spring, there stayed one night, and on departing left an old coffee-pot, some flour, etc., as proof of habitation and so gave myself the right to claim having taken possession. From there to the headquarters ranch was some thirty-five miles. On our route we came across a number of M----'s stock horses (he claimed about four to five hundred) and, taking the opportunity, we got together some 200 head, inspected them, and in this way, the only way open to me, claimed having taken possession. But now with fear and trembling we approached the ranch where M---- and his family, as I knew, were residing. A hundred yards from the house was the main spring of water, to which and at which we went and camped for dinner. Somehow or other M---- heard of our presence and out he came, a shot-gun in his hand, fury in his eyes, and his wife clinging to his coat-tails. No doubt he meant to shoot, but I was quite ready for him and put a bold face on it. Things looked nasty indeed and I was determined to fire should he once raise his gun. Perhaps this boldness made him think a bit, and I was very much relieved indeed when he resorted to expressive language instead of any more formidable demonstration. Though it was necessary to tell him that I was come to take possession of the ranch, he was not on to the affidavit game, and the result was that on returning to Fort Sumner I swore to having attempted to take possession but had been resisted by force. As explained before, such an affidavit was, in the eye of the law, a strong point in our contention of having taken possession. At least, so our legal advisers affirmed.

From Fort Sumner I then started for the round-up, taking with me a white man, the Mexican having got scared and quit. Having bought more horses, enough to fully mount two men, we joined the work. Fortunately M----'s outfit had gone up the river with a large herd of cattle, and was during their absence represented by the foreman of another ranch. What I did was to get all the foremen together (there were some ten wagons on the work) and explain to them who I was, that I was there to work and handle the M---- cattle, that if they would help me I should be obliged, but they were to understand that they would be regarded as doing it for my Company. They only said they were going to help in the usual way to gather the cattle and brand the calves; that I could work or not as I liked; that, in fact, it was none of their business as to whose the cattle were. So after working on a bit an affidavit was sent in that I had "worked" the cattle and had *met no resistance*. But mine was an extremely disagreeable position.

During this round-up I noticed that M----was carefully gathering all the steers and bulls of any age he could find. I notified my people and asked them to send the sheriff down to help me. Things were coming to a point as it were; it was evidently M----'s intention to drive the steers out of the territory, knowing that once over the Texas line we could no longer enjoin him. His whole force of men depended on this to get their wages out of these steers, as every one of them was at least three months in arrears, some of them six, twelve, and even eighteen months. Thus I knew they would make every effort to succeed in the drive and would be desperate men to interfere with. The last day of the round-up was over, and in the evening I was careful to note the direction taken by the herd.

In the meantime L---- had sent me a restraining paper to serve and I was of course determined to do it; but late that night my relief was great to see the sheriff, a Mexican, drive into camp. Here was a proper representative of the law at last, though I do not think he himself liked the job overmuch, officers of his breed being habitually treated with contempt by the white men. We agreed to take up the trail early next morning, knowing that the distance to the line was forty miles straight across the Staked Plains, no fences, no roads or trails, and no water for thirty miles at least. So up and off before daybreak, he driving a smart pair of horses, I with only my saddle pony, at as quick a gait as a wheeled vehicle could move; drove till his team began to play out, when luckily we came upon a mustang-hunter's camp and were supplied with two fresh mounts. Pushing on we at last spied in the far distance what was unmistakably a herd of cattle. Experience told me that the cattle had been watered, a fact which was thankfully noted. Watered cattle cannot be driven except at a very slow walk, and the herd was still seven or eight miles from the Texas line. M----'s foreman had made a fatal mistake! Had he not watered them they might have escaped us. They must have thought they had hoodwinked me and were probably then rejoicing at their success. They had certainly made a noble effort, having travelled all night and on till noon next day at a speed I had not thought possible. (There were even bulls in the herd.) One can imagine the feelings of the party when they at last saw us two riding at top speed directly on their trail. Cuss words must have flown freely, and no doubt the more desperate ones talked resistance. I was really anxious myself as to what course they would decide on, M---- not being with them, and they thinking of nothing but the settlement of their wages. On coming up to them they looked about as "mad" as any men could be. But they decided rightly; and seeing the game was up, merely tried to get me to promise to pay their back wages. This I would not do, but said there was time enough to talk that over afterwards; that meantime the herd must be driven back to its proper range, and to this they finally agreed. Word was brought in that M---- was lying out on the prairie, prostrated by the sun, helped no doubt by his realizing that his little scheme had been defeated. We had him brought into camp, but I declined to see him and returned to Fort Sumner. Soon afterwards M---- threw up the sponge, so to speak, and agreed to turn the property over to us. These M---- cattle, numbering only 2000, did not justify the running of a mess wagon and full outfit, so I made arrangements with a very strong neighbouring ranch company to run the cattle for us, only myself attending the round-ups to see that our interests were properly protected.

Meantime the stock horses must be looked after. Fraudulently M---- had started new brands on the last two crops of colts, the pick of them going into his wife's brand; and her mares ranged with M----'s, now ours. The band ran apparently anywhere. They had the whole Staked Plains of New Mexico to wander over, there being then absolutely no fences for a distance of 200 miles. Some 200 head of the gentler stock ranged near home; the balance, claimed to number some 300 more, were mixed up with the mustangs and were practically wild creatures, some of them having never been rounded up for over two years.

By this time some of M----'s old hands had come over to my side. They knew the country, knew how best to handle these horses, and by favourable promise I got them to undertake to help in discriminating as to which colts were the Company's property and which Mrs M----'s. So I put up an "outfit," wagon, cook, mounts for seven or eight men, etc., and set out on a very big undertaking indeed, and one that M----himself had not successfully accomplished for several years--a clean round-up of all the stock horses in the country. These Staked Plains (Llanos Estacados) were so called because the first road or trail across them had to be staked out with poles at more or less long intervals to show direction, there being no visible landmarks in that immense level country. They are one continuous sweep of slightly undulating, almost level land, well grassed, almost without living water anywhere, but dotted all over with depressions in the ground, generally circular, some of great size, some deeper than others, which we called "dry lakes," from the fact that for most of the year they were nearly all dry, only here and there, and at long distances apart, a few would hold sufficient muddy water to carry wild horses and antelope through the dry season. But which lakes held water and which not was only known to these wild mustang bands and our mares that ran with them. We took out with us some hundred of the gentler mares, the idea being to graze these round camp, and on getting round a bunch of the outlaws to drive them into this herd and so hold them. Nearly every bunch we found had mustangs amongst them. The mustang stallions we shot whenever possible. They were the cause of all our trouble. These stallions did not lead the bands, but fell behind, driving the mares in front and compelling them to gallop. When pressed, the stud would wheel round as if to challenge his pursuers. He presented a fine spectacle, his eyes blazing and his front feet pawing the ground. What a picture subject for an artist! The noble stallion, for he does look noble, no matter how physically poor a creature he may chance to be, wheeling round to challenge and threaten his pursuer, his mane and tail sweeping the ground, fury breathing from his nostrils and his eyes flashing fire! Is he not gaining time for his mares and progeny to get out of danger? A noble object and a gallant deed! Then was the time to shoot. But, yourself being all in a sweat and your horse excited, straight shooting was difficult to accomplish. We worked on a system; on finding a band, one man would do the running for six or eight miles, then another would relieve him, and so on, the idea being to get outside of them and so gradually round them in to the grazing herd. We had special horses kept and used for this purpose, fast and long-winded, as the pace had to be great and one must be utterly regardless of dog and badger holes, etc. This kind of work we kept up for a couple of weeks, some days being successful, some days getting a run but securing nothing. We made a satisfactory gathering of all the gentler and more tractable mares, but some of the wilder ones we could not hold. At night we stood guard over the band, and it was amusing, and even alarming, how the stallions would charge out and threaten any rider who approached too near his ladies. A good deal of fighting went on too between these very jealous gentlemen. As illustrating what the wild stallions are capable of, I may relate here how, one night when we had a small bunch of quite gentle mares and colts in a corral, a mustang stallion approached it, tore down the gate poles, took the mares out and forced them to his own range, some thirty miles away; and he must have driven them at a great pace, as when we followed next morning it was quite that distance before we saw any sign of them. The story is told of M---- himself who one dark night saw what he supposed was one of these depredators, shot it with his rifle, and found he had killed the only highly-bred stud he possessed.

At last we started homewards, meaning to separate the properties of the two claimants; but M---- owned the only proper horse-separating corral in the whole country, and from obstinacy and cussedness would not let us use it. Here was a pretty go! To drive to any other corral would mean taking M----'s horses off their proper range and the law forbade us doing so, and he knew it. So we were compelled to do what I reckon had never been done or attempted before--separate the horses on the open prairie! First we cut out and pushed some half a mile away all mares and young unbranded colts to which the Company's title could not be disputed; also the stallions and geldings of like nature; then came the critical and difficult part of the operation--to cut out and separate mothers from their unbranded colts, and branded colts, some even one or two years old, from their mothers. And not only cut them out, but hold them separate for a full couple of hours! No one can know what this means but one who has tried it. I had done a fair amount of yearling steer-cutting; but hard as that work is, it is nothing compared with the separating of colts from their dams. The only way was to suddenly scare the colt out and race him as hard as you could go to the other bunch. But if by bad luck its mother gave a whinny, back the colt would come like a shot bullet, and nothing on earth could stop him. Fortunately I had kept a fresh horse in reserve, a very fine fast and active cutting pony. I rode him myself, and but for him we would never have accomplished what we did. When we got through our best horses were all played out. But it was absolutely necessary to move our own mare band to the nearest corral at Fort Sumner, a distance of thirty miles, which we did that evening. To night-herd them would have been impossible. The title to many of these colts, branded and unbranded, was very much mixed up, and indeed still in the Courts. Nevertheless I prepared next morning to brand them for the Company. The fire was ready, the irons nearly hot, when up drove M----in a furious rage. I do not think I ever saw a man look so angry and mean. He held a shot-gun in his hand and, presenting it at me, swore he would kill me if I dared to proceed any further. My foreman, who knew him well, warned me to be careful; there seemed no doubt that he meant what he said; he was too mad to dispute with, and so! well, his bluff, if it were a bluff, carried the day and I ordered the mares to be turned loose. As it turned out afterwards it was well I did so, as further legal complications would have resulted. But as I began to think of and remember the time that had been spent and the amount of hard work in collecting these horses, I felt rather ashamed of my action. And yet, can one be expected to practically throw his life away, not for a principle, but for a few head of young colts not even his own property? But, as said before, the disputed title influenced me to some extent; that, and the muzzle of the shot-gun together certainly did.

A word about mustangs. They were very wary, cunning animals, keen of scent and sharp of eye. Invariably, when one first sighted them, they would be one or two miles away, going like the wind, their tails and manes flying behind them; and be it noted that when walking or standing these manes as well as tails swept the ground. Few of them were of any value when captured; many of them were so vicious and full of the devil generally that you could do nothing with them, and they never seemed to lose that character. Like the guanaco of South America, the wild stallion always dungs in one particular spot, near the watering-place, so that when hunting them we always looked out for and inspected these little hillocks. It may also be mentioned here that guanacos, like wild elephants and wild goats, have their dying ground, so to speak, where immense quantities of their bones are always found. Cattle when about to die select if possible a bush, tree or rocky place, perhaps for privacy, quietness, or some other reason unknown to us.

The next and last time we rounded up the stock horses I left the wilder ones alone, and gave a contract to some professional mustangers to gather them at so much per head. These men never attempt to run them down. They "walk" them down. A light wagon, two mules to pull it, lots of grain, some water and supplies, are what you need. On sighting a band you simply walk your team after them, walk all day and day after day, never giving them a rest. Keep their attention occupied and they will neglect to feed or drink. Gradually they become accustomed to your nearer presence, and finally you can get up quite close and even drive them into your camp, where your companions are ready with snare ropes to secure them, or at least the particular ones you want to catch.

Prince, a horse I used to ride when mustang hunting, once accidentally gave me a severe tumble. He was running at full speed when suddenly a foreleg found a deep badger hole; over he went of course, head over heels, and it is a miracle it did not break his leg off. These badger holes, especially abandoned ones, go right down to a great depth, and the grass grows over them so that they are hardly visible. Dog holes always have a surrounding pile of earth carefully patted firm and trod on, no doubt to prevent entrance of rain flood-water; thus they are nearly always noticeable. Dog towns are sometimes of great extent, one in my pasture being two miles long and about a mile wide. They are generally far from water, many miles indeed, often on the highest and driest parts of the plain and where the depth to water may be 500 feet or more. They must therefore depend entirely on the juices of the green grass, though in dry seasons they cannot even have that refreshment; and they never scrape for roots. But even the small bunnies (called cotton-tails) are found in like places and must subsist absolutely without water, as they do not, or dare not, on account of wolves, etc., get far away from their holes.

No sooner was the M---- trouble well over than my Company saw fit to foreclose on two other cattle outfits, one of which bowed to the law at once. The other gave us, or rather me, a lot of unnecessary trouble, and I had again "to take chances" of personal injury. All these cattle were thrown on to the M---- range, and this increased the herd so much as to justify the running of our own wagon and outfit.

Eastern New Mexico, the country over which our cattle ranged, was a huge strip of territory some 250 miles by 100 miles, no fences, no settlers, occupied only by big cattle outfits owning from 8000 to 75,000 cattle each. The range was, however, much too heavily stocked, the rains irregular, severe droughts frequent, and the annual losses yearly becoming heavier; so heavy in fact that owners only waited a slight improvement in prices to sell out or drive their cattle out of the country. The way the cattle were worked was thus. The spring round-up began in March, far down the river, and slowly worked north to our range. Our wagon, one of many more, would join the work some 110 miles south of our range, but I sent individual men to much greater distances. The work continued slowly through the range, branding the spring calves, and each outfit separating its own cattle and driving its own herd. Twelve or more wagons meant some 300 riders and about 3000 saddle horses. So the operation was done on a grand scale; thousands of cattle were handled every day, and altogether such a big round-up was a very busy and interesting scene. Intricate and complicated work it was, too, though not perhaps apparent to an outsider; but under a good round-up boss, who was placed over the bosses of all the wagons, it was wonderful how smoothly the work went on. A general round-up took a long time and was no sooner over than another was begun at the far south border (the Mexico line) and the thing repeated. Our own cattle had got into the habit of drifting south whenever winter set in. It took us all summer to get them

HERD ON TRAIL. SHOWING LEAD STEER.

back again, and no sooner back than a cold sleet or rain would start them south. In fact, in winter few of our own cattle were at home, the cattle on our range being then mostly those drifted from the northern part of the territory. Such were the conditions in a "free range" country, and these conditions broke nearly all these big outfits, or at least compelled them to market their stuff for whatever it would bring. Partly on account of long-drawnout lawsuits we held on for seven or eight years, when on a recovery of prices our Company also closed out its live-stock interests. During the turning-over of these, the Company's cattle, to the purchasers, of course they had to be all branded, not with a recorded brand, but simply with a tally brand, thus , on the hip. Had there been a convenient separate pasture to put the tallied cattle into as they were tallied, much work would have been saved and no opportunity offered for fraud, such as will now be suggested and explained. The method adopted was to begin gathering at one end of the range, tally the herd collected, and then necessarily turn them loose. But we had bad stormy weather and these tallied cattle drifted and scattered all over the country and mixed up with those still not rounded up. This at once gave the opportunity for an evilly-inclined man to do just as was soon rumoured and reported to me. It was even positively asserted to me by certain cowmen (this was while I was confined in bed from an accident) that the buyer had a gang of men out operating on the far end of the range, catching and tally-branding for him the still untallied cattle. A simple operation enough, in such an immense district, where four men with their ropes could, in a few undisturbed days' work, cheat the Company out of enough cattle at $20 a head to be well worth some risk. Several men were positive in their assertions to me. But I knew these gentlemen pretty well--cattle-thieves themselves and utterly unprincipled; perhaps having a grudge against the said buyer, perhaps wanting merely to annoy me, and also possibly hating to see such a fine opportunity not taken advantage of. In the end, when brought to the scratch, not one of these informers would testify under oath. Whether afraid to, as they would undoubtedly have run strong chances of being killed, or whether they were just mischief-makers, as I myself have always believed, it is impossible to know accurately. The buyer, being a man of means and having many other interests in the district, would certainly hesitate long before he took such a very dangerous risk of discovery. All that can be said about it is that though I employed detectives for some time to try to get evidence bearing on the subject, no such evidence was ever obtained. The shortage in the turnover was due simply to the usual miscalculation of the herd; the herd which never before had been counted and could not, under range conditions, be counted.

These were still "trailing" days, which means that steers sold or for sale were driven out of the country, not shipped by rail cars. One great trail passed right through our ranch (a great nuisance too), and by it herd after herd, each counting, maybe, 2500 cattle, was continually being trailed northwards, some going to Kansas or the Panhandle, most of them going as far north as Nebraska, Wyoming and Montana. These latter herds would be on the trail continuously for two or three months. Our own steers were always driven to the Panhandle of Texas, where, if not already contracted to buyers, they were held till sold.

A herd of breeding-stock when on the trail must be accompanied by one or more calf wagons, wagons with beds well boxed up, in which the youngest or new-born calves are carried, they being lifted out and turned over to their mother's care at night or during stoppages. In the old days, when such calves had no value, they were knocked on the head or carelessly and cruelly abandoned.

It is a strange fact to note that when a herd is on the trail there is always a particular steer which, day after day and week after week, occupies a self-assigned position at the head of the herd, and is therefore called the "lead steer." I have often wondered what his thoughts might be, if any; why he so regularly placed himself at the head of affairs and was apparently so jealous of his commanding position. Yes, the lead steer is a mysterious creature, yet if displaced by death or some such cause, another long-legged, keen traveller will at once take his place. It should be explained that a herd on the trail travels naturally best in an extended form, two deep, seldom more than three or six, except towards the tail end, called the "drag": so that a herd of 2000 steers will form a much-attenuated line a mile in length from one end to the other.

Which reminds me of an incident in this connection. I was moving a small lot of steers, some 400 head in all, to pasture in the Panhandle of Texas. The force consisted only of the wagon driver, one cowboy and myself. But the cowboy turned out to be quite ignorant of the art of driving cattle, did more harm than good, and so annoyed me that I dismissed him to the rear to ride in the wagon if he so chose, and myself alone undertook to drive, or rather not so much to drive, that being hardly necessary, as to guide the herd on its course. I got them strung out beautifully half a mile long, and they were making good time, when suddenly a confounded sheep herder and his dog met the lead steers and the procession was at once a scene of the most utter confusion. It should be explained here that, in the case of a small herd thus strung out, its guidance, if left to only one man, may be done from the rear by simply riding out sharply to one side or the other and calling to the lead cattle. How I did curse that wretch and his dog. A man on foot was bad enough; but a man on foot with a dog! Horrors! Yet, perhaps, barring the delay in getting the cattle started again, the incident had its uses, as it had just previously occurred to me that the line was getting a bit too long and might soon be out of control. Such are the uses of adversity.

It can be understood that even a small herd of 400 lusty young steers can keep a man, or even two or three men, busy enough, especially if there are any cattle on the range you are passing through. In this case there were fortunately few.

Amarillo, being the southern end of the Kansas railroad, was a great cattle market. Buyers and sellers met there; and there, immediately around the town, were congregated at any time in spring as many as 40,000 cattle, all under herd. Amarillo was then the greatest cattle town in the world. She was the successor of such towns as Wichita and Fort Dodge, simply because she was at the western terminus of the railway. Though a pretty rowdy town her manners were an improvement on such places as Dodge, where in the height of her wickedness a gambling dispute, rivalry for the smile of a woman, or the slightest discourtesy, was sufficient ground for the shedding of blood.

My life during these eight years had its pleasures and its troubles; certainly much discomfort and a lot of disagreeable work. During the working season, April to November, my time was mostly spent with the round-up or on the trail, with occasional visits to our head office in Las Vegas, and also to Amarillo on business matters. To cover these immense distances, near 300 miles (there were few or no desirable stopping-places), I used a light spring wagon or ambulance, holding my bedding, mess-box, grain for the team, some water, stake ropes, and a hundred other things. I nearly always camped out on the prairie, of course cooked my own meals, was out in all kinds of weather--sun, rain, heat and drought, blizzards and frightful lightning storms. My favourite team was a couple of grey ponies. From being so much together we got to understand each other pretty thoroughly, and we had our adventures as well. Once on going up a very steep hill the ponies lost their footing. The wagon backed and turned over, and ponies and wagon rolled over and over down the hill among the rocks till hung up on a cedar stump. I was not much hurt, but found the ponies half covered with stones and rocks that had rolled on to them, the wagon upside down and camping material scattered everywhere. Cutting the tugs and rolling the stones away the ponies jumped up miraculously little injured, and even the wagon still serviceable, but I had to walk a long way to get assistance. Then we have fallen through rotten bridges, stuck in rivers and quicksands, and all sorts of things.

One pony of this team, "Punch," was really the hardiest, best-built, best-natured and most intelligent of any I have ever known. Many a time, on long trips, has the other pony played completely out and actually dropped on the road. But Punch seemed to be never tired. He was a great pet too, and could be fondled to your heart's content. He had no vice, yet was as full of mischief as he could possibly pack. His mischief, or rather playfulness, finally cost him his life, as he once got to teasing a bull, the bull charged, and that was his end.

It was with this team too that when driving in New Mexico through a district where white men were seldom seen, but on a road which I had often selected as a shorter route to my destination, I came on a Mexican ill-treating his donkey. His actions were so deliberate as to rouse my ire, and I got down, took the club from him and threatened castigation. On proceeding on the road I passed another Mexican mounted on a horse and carrying a rifle. Happening by-and-by to look back much was my surprise, or perhaps not very much, to see the gun and horse handed over to the first man, and himself mounted and galloping after me. Knowing at once what it meant, that his game was to bushwhack me in the rough canon immediately in front, I put the whip to my team to such good purpose that we galloped through that canon as it had never been galloped through before. I would have had no show whatever in such a place, and so was extremely glad to find myself again in the open country.

Another time I hitched up another team, one of which, a favourite mustang-chaser, had never been driven. We made some ten miles all right till we came to the "jumping-off" place of the plains, a very steep, long and winding descent. Just as we started down, Prince, the horse mentioned, got his tail over the lines, and the ball began. We went down that hill at racing speed, I having absolutely no control over the terrified animals, which did not stop for many miles. Again, with the same team I once started to Amarillo, being half a day ahead of the steer herd. First evening I camped out at a water-hole and staked out Prince with a long heavy rope and strong iron stake pin. The other horse was hobbled with a rope hobble. Some wolves came in to water, and I was lying on my bed looking at them when the horses suddenly stampeded, the strong stake rope and pin not even checking Prince. They were gone and I was afoot! Prince ran for forty miles to the ranch. The hobbled horse we never saw again for more than twelve months, but when found was fat and none the worse. Next day the trail outfit came along and so I hitched up another team.

But the worst trouble I used to have was with a high-strung and almost intractable pair of horses, Pintos, or painted, which means piebald, a very handsome team indeed, whose former owner simply could not manage them. Every time we came to a gate through which we had to pass I, being alone, had to get down and throw the gate open. Then after taking the team through I had of course to go back to shut the gate again. Then was the opportunity apparently always watched for by these devils, and had I not tied a long rope to the lines and trailed it behind the wagon they would many times have succeeded in getting away.

Yet it is only such a team that one can really care to drive for pleasure; a team that you "feel" all the time, one that will keep you "interested" every minute, as these Pintos did. How often nowadays does one ever see a carriage pair, or fours in the park or elsewhere that really needs "driving"?

"Shipping" cattle means loading them into railroad cars and despatching them to their destination. The cattle are first penned in a corral and then run through chutes into the cars. One year I sold the Company's steers, a train-load, to a Jew dealer in Kansas. They were loaded in the Panhandle and I went through with them, having a man to help me to look after them, our duty being to prod them up when any were found lying down so they would not be trodden to death. At a certain point our engine "played out" and was obliged to leave us to get coal and water. While gone the snow (a furious blizzard was blowing) blew over the track and blocked it so effectively that the engine could not get back. The temperature was about zero and the cattle suffered terribly; but there we remained stuck for nearly two days.

When we finally got through, of course the buyer refused to receive them, and I turned them over to the railway company and brought suit for their value. The case was thrice tried and we won each time; and oh, how some of these railroad men did damn themselves by perjury! But it is bad business to "buck" against a powerful railway corporation. This will serve to give an idea as to what shipping cattle means. Many hundreds of thousands, or even millions, are now shipped every year. Trail work is abandoned, being no longer possible on account of fences, etc. Such great towns as Chicago and Kansas City will each receive and dispose of in one day as many as ten to twenty thousand cattle, not counting sheep or hogs.

It was when returning to Amarillo after this trip that I was fortunate enough to save the lives of a whole train-load of people. One night our passenger train came to a certain station, and the conductor went to get his orders. Nearly all the passengers were asleep. When he returned I happened to hear him read his orders over to the brakeman. These orders were to go on to a certain switch and "side track" till *three* cattle trains had passed. At that point there was a very heavy grade and cattle trains came down it at sixty miles an hour. Two trains swung past us, and to my surprise the conductor then gave the signal to go ahead. We did start, when I at once ventured to remark to him that only two trains had so far gone by. He pooh-poohed my assertion; but after a few minutes began to think that he himself might just possibly be wrong. Meantime I got out on the platform and was ready to jump. The conductor most fortunately reversed the order, and the train was backed on to the siding again, none too soon, for just then the head-light of the third cattle train appeared round a curve and came tearing past us. It was a desperately narrow escape and I did not sleep again that night. Writing afterwards to the general manager of the railway company about it my letter was not even acknowledged, and of course no thanks were received.

While on the subject of railroad accidents it has been my misfortune to have been in many of them, caused by collisions, spreading of rails, open switches, etc., etc., but I will only detail one or two. Once when travelling to Amarillo from a Convention at Fort Worth the train was very crowded and I occupied an upper berth in the Pullman. As American trains are always doing, trying to make up lost time, we were going at a pretty good lick when I felt the coach begin to sway. It swayed twice and then turned completely over and rolled down a high embankment. Outside was pitch dark and raining. There was a babel of yells and screams and callings for help. I had practically no clothes on, no shoes, and of course could find nothing. Everything inside, mattresses, bedding, curtains, baggage, clothing, babies, women and men were mixed up in an extraordinary way. Above me I noticed a broken window, through which I managed to scramble, and on finding out how things were returned to the coach to help other passengers. Underneath me seemed to be a dying man. He was in a dreadful condition and at his last gasp, etc., and he made more row than the rest put together. Reaching down and removing mattresses, he grasped my hand, jumped up and thanked me profusely for *saving* his life. He was not hurt a bit, indeed was the only man in the lot who escaped serious injury. The men behaved much worse than the women. However we soon had everybody out and the injured laid on blankets. Meantime a relief train had arrived with the doctor, etc. He examined us all, asked me if I was all right, to which I replied that I was, as I really felt so at the time. But in half an hour I was myself lying on a stretcher and unable to move, with a sprained back and bruised side, etc., and a claim for damages against the railway company.

Another time, when riding in the caboose (the rear car) of a long freight train, with the conductor and brakeman, the train in going down a grade broke in three. The engine and a few cars went right on and left us; the centre part rushed down the hill, our section followed and crashed into it, and some seven or eight cars were completely telescoped. I had been seated beside the stove, my arm stretched round it, when, noticing our great speed, I drew the conductor's attention to it. He opened the side door to look out. Just then the shock came and he got a frightful lick on the side of the head, and myself was thrown on top of the hot stove; but none of us were seriously hurt.

Again, once when making a trip to Kansas City and back, the whole Pullman train went off the track and down the embankment; and on the return journey we ran into an open switch and were derailed and one man killed. Both might have been very serious affairs.

With the closing out of the Mortgage Company's interests of course my salaried employment came to an end. But before closing this chapter it should be mentioned that I had in the meantime suffered a nasty accident by a pony falling back on me and fracturing one leg. It occurred at the round-up, and I was driven some thirty miles, the leg

not even splinted or put in a box, to my ranch. I sent off a mounted man to Las Vegas, 130 miles, for a surgeon, but it was a week before he got down to me and the leg was then in a pretty bad shape. He hinted at removing it, but finally decided to set it and put it in plaster, which he did. He then left me. The leg gave me little trouble, but unfortunately peritonitis set in. The agony then suffered will not soon be forgotten. There was a particularly ignorant woman, my foreman's wife, in the house; but I had practically no nursing, no medicine of any kind, and the diet was hardly suited for a patient. The pain became so great that I was not able to open my mouth, dared not move a muscle, and was reduced to a mere skeleton. Then it occurred to my "guardians" to send once more for the doctor. Another week went by, and when he came I had just succeeded in passing the critical stage and was on the mend. In after years this attack led to serious complications and a most interesting operation, which left me, in my doctor's words, "practically without a stomach"; and without a stomach I have jogged on comfortably for nearly ten years. How a little thing may lead to serious consequences! I had previously, and have since, had more or less serious physical troubles, but a good sound constitution has always pulled me through safely. Among minor injuries may be mentioned a broken rib, a knee-cap damaged at polo, and another slightly-fractured leg, caused again by a pony just purchased, and being tried, falling back on me; not to mention the *sigillum diavoli* (don't be alarmed or shocked) which occasionally develops, and always at the same spot.

While the round-up and turnover of the Company's cattle was proceeding, I thought it well to keep lots of whisky on hand to show hospitality (the only way) to whomsoever it was due. On receiving a large keg of it I put it in my buggy and drove out of camp seven or eight miles to some rough ground, and having, in Baden-Powell way, made myself sure no one was in view and no one spying on my movements I placed it amongst some rocks and brush in such a way that no ordinary wanderer could possibly see it. From this store it was my intention to fill a bottle every other day and so always have a stock on hand. But Kronje or De Wett was too "slim" for me; a few days afterwards on my going there, like a thief in the night--and indeed it was at night--I found the keg gone. Someone must have loaded up on it, someone who had deliberately watched me, and his joy can be easily pictured. So someone was greatly comforted, but not a hint ever came to me as to who the culprit was.

My intercourse with M---- provided some of the closest "calls" I ever had (a call means a position of danger); still not so close as on a certain occasion, at my summer camp in Arizona, when one of the men and myself were playing cards together. We were alone. The man was our best "hand," and a capital fellow, though a fugitive from justice, like some of the others. It became apparent to me that he was cheating, and I was rash enough to let him understand that I knew it, without however absolutely accusing him of it. At once he pulled out his gun, leant over, and pointed it at me. What can one do in such a case? He had the "drop" on me; and demanded that I should take back what I had said. Well, I wriggled out of it somehow, told him he was very foolish to make such a "break" as that, and talked to him till he cooled down. It was an anxious few minutes, and I am very proud to think he did not "phase" me very much, as he afterwards admitted. Peace was secured with honour.

I was lucky to be able to leave the West and the cattle business with a hide free from perforations and punctures of any kind.

CHAPTER VI
ODDS AND ENDS

Summer Round-up Notes--Night Guarding--Stampedes--Bronco Busting--Cattle Branding, etc.

Round-up and trail work had many agreeable aspects, and though it was at times very hard work, still I look back to it all with fond memories. The hours were long--breakfast was already cooked and "chuck" called long before sunrise; horses were changed, the night horses turned loose and a fresh mount for the morning's work caught out of the ramuda. By the time breakfast was over it was generally just light enough to see dimly the features of the country. The boss then gave his orders to the riders as to where to go and what country to round-up, also the round-up place at noon. He started the day-herd off grazing towards the same place, and finally saw the wagon with its four mules loaded up and despatched. There was generally a "circus" every morning on the men starting out to their work. On a cold morning a cow-horse does not like to be very tightly cinched or girthed up. He resents it by at once beginning to buck furiously as soon as his rider gets into his saddle.

Even staid old horses will do it on a very cold morning. But the "young uns," the broncos, are then perfect fiends. Thus there is nearly always some sport to begin the day with. By noon the round-up has been completed and a large herd of cattle collected. Separating begins at once, first cows and calves, then steers and "dry" cattle, the property of the different owners represented. Dinner is ready by twelve, horses changed again and the day-herd is watered, and then the branding of the calves begins. But wait. *Such* a dinner! With few appliances it is really wonderful how a mess-wagon cook feeds the crowd so well. His fuel is "chips" (*bois des vaches*); with a spade he excavates a sunken fireplace, and over this erects an iron rod on which to hang pots, etc. He will make the loveliest fresh bread and rolls at least once a day, often twice; make most excellent coffee (and what a huge coffee-pot is needed for twenty or thirty thirsty cowpunchers), serve potatoes, stewed or fried meat, baked beans and stewed dried fruit, etc. Everything was good, so cleanly served and served so quickly. True, any kind of a mess tastes well to the hungry man, but I think that even a dyspeptic's appetite would become keen when he approached the cattleman's chuck wagon. Dinner over the wagon is again loaded up, the twenty or more beds thrown in, the team hitched and started for the night camping-ground, some place where there is lots of good grass for the cattle and saddle horses, and at the same time far enough away from all the other herds. The saddle horses in charge of the horse "wrangler" accompany the wagon. The men are either grazing and drifting the day-herd towards the camp, or branding morning calves, not in a corral but on the open prairie. The calves, and probably some grown cattle to be branded, must be caught with the rope, and here is where the roper's skill is shown to most advantage. At sundown all the men have got together again, night horses are selected, supper disposed of, beds prepared and a quiet smoke enjoyed.

If a horse-hair rope be laid on the ground around one's bed no snake will ever cross it. But during work the beds are seldom made down till after sunset, by which time rattlesnakes have all retired into holes or amongst brush, and so there is little danger from them.

First "guard" goes out to take charge of the herd. The herd has already been "bedded" down carefully at convenient distance from the wagon. Bedding down means bunching them together very closely, just leaving them enough room to lie down comfortably. They, if they have been well grazed and watered, will soon all be lying resting, chewing their cuds and at peace with the world. Each night-guard consists of two to four men according to the size of the herd, and "stands" two to four hours. The horse herd is also guarded by "reliefs." In fine weather it is no great hardship to be called out at any hour of the night, but if it should be late in autumn and snow falling, or, what is worse still, if there be a cold rain and a bitter wind it is very trying to be compelled to leave your warm bed at twelve or three in the morning, get on to your poor shivering horse and stand guard for three hours.

CHANGING HORSES.

It should be explained that "standing" means not absolute inaction but slowly riding round and round the herd. Yes, it is trying, especially in bad weather and after working hard all day long from before sun-up. How well one gets to know the stars and their positions! The poor night-herders know that a certain star will set or be in such and such a position at the time for the next relief. Often when dead tired, sleepy and cold, how eagerly have I watched my own star's apparently very slow movement. The standard watch is at the wagon, and must not be "monkeyed" with, a trick sometimes played on tenderfeet. Immediately time for relief is up the next is called, and woe betide them if they delay complying with the summons. Of course the owner or manager does not have to take part in night-herding, but the boys think more of him if he does, and certainly the man he relieves appreciates it.

In continued wet and cold weather such as we were liable to have late in October or November, when it might rain and drizzle for a week or two at a time, our beds would get very wet and there would be no sun to dry them.

Consequently we practically slept in wet, not damp, blankets for days at a time; and to return from your guard about two in the morning and get into such an uninviting couch was trying to one's temper, of course. Even one's "goose haar piller," as the boys called their feather pillow, might be sodden. To make your bed in snow or be snowed over is not nearly so bad.

No tents were ever seen on the round-up. Everyone slept on the open bare ground. But for use during my long drives across country I got to using a small Sibley tent, nine feet by nine feet, which had a canvas floor attached to the walls, and could be closed up at night so as to effectually prevent the entrance of skunks and other vermin. This tent had no centre pole whatever. You simply drove in the four corner stake-pins, raised the two light rods over it triangularwise, and by a pulley and rope hoist up the peak. The two rods were very thin, light and jointed; and in taking the tent down you simply loosed the rope, knocked out the stake-pins, and that was all.

During these long guarding spells you practically just sit in your saddle for four hours at a stretch. You cannot take exercise and you dare not get down to walk or you will stampede the cattle. But, yes, you may gallop to camp if you know the direction, and drink a cup of hot strong coffee, which in bad weather is kept on the fire all night, re-light your pipe and return to "sing" to the cattle.

Then the quiet of these huge animals is impressive. About midnight they will get a bit restless, many will get on their feet, have a stretch and a yawn, puff, cough and blow and in other ways relieve themselves, and if allowed will start out grazing; but they are easily driven back and will soon be once more resting quietly.

The stampeding of the herd on such a night is almost a relief. It at once effectually wakes you up, gets you warm, and keeps you interested for the rest of your spell, even if it does not keep you out for the rest of the night.

I should explain that "singing" to the cattle refers to the habit cowboys have, while on night-guard, of singing (generally a sing-song refrain) as they slowly ride round the herd. It relieves the monotony, keeps the cattle quiet and seems to give them confidence, for they certainly appear to rest quieter while they know that men are guarding them, and are not so liable to stampede.

Stampeding is indeed a very remarkable bovine characteristic. Suppose a herd of cattle, say 2000 steers, to be quietly and peacefully lying down under night-guard. The air is calm and clear. It may be bright moonlight, or it may be quite dark; nothing else is moving. Apparently there is nothing whatever to frighten them or even disturb them; most of them are probably sound asleep, when suddenly like a shot they, the whole herd, are on their feet and gone--gone off at a more or less furious gallop. All go together. The guard are of course at once all action; the men asleep in camp are waked by the loud drumming of the thousands of hoofs on the hard ground and at once rush for their horses to assist. The stampede must be stopped and there is only one way to do it--to get up to the lead animals and try to swing them round with the object of getting them to move in a circle, to "mill" as we called it. But the poor beasts meantime are frantic with fear and excitement and you must ride hard at your level best, and look out you don't get knocked over and perhaps fatally trampled on. You must know your business and work on one plan with your fellow-herders. On a pitch dark night in a rough country it is very dangerous indeed. The cattle may run only a short distance or they may run ten miles, and after being quieted again may once more stampede. Indeed, I took a herd once to Amarillo and they stampeded the first night on the trail and kept it up pretty near every night during the drive. But, as said before, the remarkable part of the performance is the instantaneous nature of the shock or whatever it is that goes through the slumbering herd, and the quickness of their getting off the bed-ground.

Cow and calf herds are not so liable to stampede, but horses are distinctly bad and will run for miles at terrific speed. Then you must just try and stay with them and bring them back when they stop, as you can hardly expect to outrun them. Still, I do not think that stampeded horses are quite so crazy as cattle, and they get over their fright quicker.

Let me try to illustrate a little better an actual stampede. The night was calm, clear, but very dark--no moon, and the stars dimmed by fleecy cloud strata. The herd of some 2000 steers was bedded down, and had so far given no trouble. Supper was over and the first guard on duty, the rest of the men lying on their beds chatting and smoking. Each man while not on duty has his saddled horse staked close by. Soon everyone has turned in for the night. A couple of hours later the first guard come in, their spell being over, and the second relief takes their place. The cattle are quiet; not a sound breaks the silence except the low crooning of some of the boys on duty. But suddenly, what is that noise?--like the distant rumbling of guns on the march, or of a heavy train crossing a wooden bridge! To one with his head on the ground the earth seems almost to tremble. Oh, we know it well! It is the beating of 8000 hoofs on the hard ground. The cowboy recognizes the dreaded sound instantly: it wakens him quicker than anything else. The boss is already in his saddle, has summoned the other men, and is off at full gallop. The cook gets up, re-trims his lamp, and hangs it as high on the wagon top as he can, to be visible as far as possible. It is good two miles before we catch up on the stampeded herd, still going at a mad gallop. The men are on flank trying to swing them round. But someone seems to be in front, as we soon can hear pistol-shots fired in a desperate endeavour to stop the lead steers. But even that is no avail, and indeed is liable to split the herd in two and so double the work. So the thundering race continues, and it is only after many miles have been covered that the cattle have run themselves out and we finally get them quietened down and turned homewards. Someone is sent out scouting round to try to get a view of the cook's lantern and so know our whereabouts. But have we got all the cattle? The men are questioned. Where's Pete? and where's Red? There must be cattle gone and these two men are staying with them. Well, we'll take the herd on anyway, bed them down again, get fresh horses, and then hunt up the missing bunch. So, the cattle once more "bedded," and every spare hand left with them, as they are liable to run again, two of us start out to find if possible the missing men.

We first take a careful note of the position of any stars that may be visible, then start out at an easy lope or canter. It is so dark that it seems a hopeless task to find them. Good luck alone may guide us right; and good luck serves us well, for after having come some eight or nine miles we hear a man "hollering" to us. He had heard our horses' tread, and was no doubt mightily relieved at our coming, as of course he was completely lost in the darkness and had wisely not made any attempt to find his way. But there he was, good fellow, Red! with his little bunch of 200 steers. Yes, the herd had split, that's how it was. But where is Pete? Oh! he doesn't know; last saw him heading the stampede; never saw him since. Can he be lost and still wandering round? That is not likely, and we begin to suspect trouble. The small herd is directed campwards, and some of us again scout round, halloing and shouting, but keeping our eyes well "skinned" for anything on the ground. At last, by the merest chance, we come on something; no doubt what it is--the body of a man. "Hallo, Pete! What's the matter?" He stirs. "Are you badly hurt?" "Dog-gone it, fellows, glad to see you! My horse fell and some cattle ran over me. No! I ain't badly hurt; but I guess you'll have to carry me home." The poor fellow had several ribs broken, was dreadfully bruised, and his left cheek was nearly sliced off. There we had to leave him till morning, one of us staying by. Happily Pete got all right again.

Breaking young colts was a somewhat crude process. Not being of the same value as better bred stock they were rather roughly treated. If you have a number to break you will hire a professional "bronco-buster"; for some five dollars a head he will turn them back to you in a remarkably short time, bridle-wise, accustomed to the saddle and fairly gentle. But he does not guarantee against pitching. Some colts never pitch at all during the process, do not seem to know how; but the majority do know, and know well! The colt is roped in a corral by the forefeet, jerked down, and his head held till bridled; or he is roped round the neck, snubbed to a post and so held till he chokes himself by straining on the running loop. As soon as he falls a man jumps on to his head and holds it firmly in such a way that he cannot get up, and someone slips on the Hackamore bridle. Thus you will see that a horse lying on its side requires his muzzle as a lever to get him on his feet. Then he is allowed to rise and to find, though he may not then realize it, that his wild freedom is gone from him for ever. He is trembling with fright and excitement, and sweating from every pore. To get the saddle on him he is next blindfolded. A strong man grasps the left ear and another man slowly approaches and, after quietly and kindly rubbing and patting him, gently puts the saddle blanket in place; then the huge and heavy saddle with all its loose strings and straps is carefully hoisted and adjusted, and the cinch drawn up. In placing the blanket and the saddle there will likely be several failures. He will be a poor-spirited horse that does not resent it. Now take off the blinders and let him pitch till he is tired. Then comes the mounting. He is blinded again, again seized by the ear, the cinch pulled very tight, and the rider mounts into the saddle. It may be best first to lead him outside the corral, so that he can run right off with his man if he wants to. But he won't run far, as he soon exhausts himself in his rage and with his tremendous efforts to dismount his rider. A real bad one will squeal like a pig, fall back, roll over, kick and apparently tie himself into knots. If mastered the first time it is a great advantage gained. But should he throw his rider once, twice or several times he never forgets that the thing is at least possible, and so he may repeat his capers for a long time to come. All cow-horses have ever afterwards a holy dread of the rope, never forgetting its power and effect experienced during the breaking process. Thus, in roping a broken horse on the open or in a corral, if your rope simply lies *over* his neck, and yet not be round it, he will probably stop running and resign himself to capture. Even the commonly-used single rope corral, held up by men at the corners, they will not try to break through. Bronco-busters only last a few years, the hard jarring affects their lungs and other organs so disastrously.

One of our men, with the kindest consideration, much appreciated, confidentially showed me a simple method of tying up a bronco's head with a piece of thin rope, adjusted in a particular way, which made pitching or bucking almost, but not always, an impossibility. He was perhaps a little shamefaced in doing so, but such sensibility was not for me; anything to save one from the horrible shaking up and jarring of a pitching horse! And yet there was always the inclination to fix the string surreptitiously. Much better that the boys should *not* see it.

It may be said here that a horse has a lightning knowledge as to whether his rider be afraid of him or not, and acts accordingly. In branding my method was to simply tie up one forefoot and blindfold the colt, when a small and properly-hot stamp-iron can be quickly and effectively applied before he quite knows what is hurting him.

A REAL BAD ONE.

In early days we used only Spanish Mexican broncos for cow-ponies. They were broken bridle-wise, and perhaps had been ridden a few times. Bands of them were driven north to our country, and for about fifteen dollars apiece you might make a selection of the number wanted, say twenty to fifty head. Some of these ponies would turn out very well, some of little use. You took your chances, and in distributing them amongst the men very critical eyes were cast over them, you may be sure, as the boys had to ride them no matter what their natures might turn out to be. Such ponies were hardy, intelligent, active, and stood a tremendous amount of work. Later a larger stamp of cow-horse came into use, even horses with perhaps a distant and minute drop of Diomede's blood in them--Diomede, who won the first Derby stakes, run for in the Isle of Man by the way, and who was sold to America to become the father of United States thoroughbreds and progenitor of the great Lexington. But such "improved" horses could never do the cow work so well as the old original Spanish cayuse.

In a properly-organized cattle country all cattle brands must be recorded at the County seat. Because of the prodigious number and variety of brands of almost every conceivable pattern and device it is difficult to adopt a quite new and safe one that does not conflict in some way with others. This for the honest man; the crooked man, the thief, the brand-burner is not so troubled. *He* will select a brand such as others already in use may be easily changed into. To give a very few instances. If his own brand be 96 and another's 91 the conversion is easy. If it be [**#] and another's [**-II-] it is equally easy; or if it be [**3--E], as was one of our own brands, the conversion of it into [**d--B] is too temptingly simple. It was only after much consideration that I adopted for my own personal brand [**U]--a mule shoe on the left hip and jaw. It was small and did not damage the hide too much, was easily stamped on, looked well and was pretty safe. Among brands I have seen was HELL in large letters covering the animal's whole side.

With a band of horses a bell-mare (madrina) is sometimes used. The mare is gentle, helps to keep the lot together, and the bell lets you know on a dark night where they are. With a lot of mules a madrina is always used, as her charges will never leave her.

All the grooming cow-ponies get is self-administered. After a long ride, on pulling the saddle off, the pony is turned loose, when he at once proceeds to roll himself from one side to another, finishing up with a "shake" before he goes off grazing. If he has been overridden he may not succeed in rolling completely over. This is regarded as a sure sign that he has been overridden, and you know that he will take some days, or even maybe weeks, to recover from it. I have seen horses brought in absolutely staggering and trembling and so turned loose. A favourite mount is seldom so mistreated; and if the boss is present the rider knows he will take a note of it. One can imagine how delightful and refreshing this roll and shake must be, quite as refreshing as a cold bath (would be) to the tired and perspiring rider. Alas! cold or hot baths are not obtainable by the cattleman for possibly months at a time. The face and hands alone can receive attention. The new and modern idea of bodily self-cleansing is here effectually put in force and apparently with good health results. The rivers when in flood are extremely muddy; when not they are very shallow, and the water is usually alkaline and undrinkable, as well as quite useless for bathing purposes.

Cow-ponies generally have sound feet and durable hoofs, but in very sandy countries the hoofs will spread out in a most astonishing way and need constant trimming.

In droughty countries like Arizona and New Mexico we were frequently reduced to serious straits to find decent drinking-water. On many occasions I have drunk, and drunk with relief and satisfaction, such filthy, slimy, greenish-looking stuff as would disgust a frog and give the *Lancet* a fit, though that discriminating journal would probably call it soup. Sometimes even water, and I well remember the places, that was absolutely a struggling mass of small red creatures that yet really tasted not at all badly. Anyway it was better than the green slime. Thirst is a sensation that must be satisfied at any cost. Once when travelling in the South Arizona country, we being all strung out in Indian file, over a dozen of us, the lead man came on a most enticing-looking pool of pure water. Of course he at once jumped off, took a hearty draught, spat it out and probably made a face, but saying nothing rode quietly on. The next man did the same, and so it went on till our predecessors had each and all the satisfaction of knowing that he was not the only man fooled. The water was so hot, though showing no sign of it, that it was quite undrinkable--a very hot spring.

In the alkali district on the Pecos River the dust raised at a round-up is so dense that the herd cannot even be seen at 200 yards distance. This dust is most irritating to the eyes; and many of the men, including myself, were sometimes so badly affected that they had to stop work for weeks at a time.

In circuses and Wild-West shows one frequently sees cowgirls on the bill. Of course, on actual work on the range there is no such thing as a cowgirl. At least I never saw one.

CHAPTER VII
ON MY OWN RANCH

Locating--Plans--Prairie Fires an Guards--Bulls--Trading--Successful Methods--Loco-weed--Sale of Ranch.

A year before selling out the Company's cattle I had started a small ranch for myself. Seeing that it was quite hopeless to run cattle profitably on the open-range system, and having longing eyes on a certain part of the plains which was covered with very fine grass and already fenced on one side by the Texas line--knowing also quite well that fencing of public land in New Mexico was strictly against the law (land in the territories is the property of the Federal Government, which will neither lease it nor sell it, but holds it for home-steading)--I yet went to work, bought a lot of wire and posts, gave a contract to a fence-builder and boldly ran a line over thirty miles long enclosing something like 100,000 acres. The location was part of the country where our stock horses used to run with the mustangs, and so I knew every foot of it pretty well. There was practically no limit to the acreage I might have enclosed; and I had then the choice of all sorts of country--country with lots of natural shelter for cattle, and even country where water in abundance could be got close to the surface. In my selected territory I knew quite well that it was very deep to water and that it would cost a lot of money in the shape of deep wells and powerful windmills to get it out; yet it was for this very reason that I so selected it. Would not the country in a few years swarm with settlers ("nesters" as we called small farmers), and would they not of course first select the land where water was shallow? They could not afford to put in expensive wells and windmills. Thus I argued, and thus it turned out exactly as anticipated. The rest of the country became settled up by these nesters, but I was left alone for some eight years absolutely undisturbed and in complete control of this considerable block of land. More than that the County Assessor and collector actually missed me for two years, not even knowing of my existence; and for the whole period of eight years I never paid one cent for rent. On my windmill locations I put "Scrip" in blocks of forty acres. Otherwise I owned or rented not a foot.

Just a line or two here. I happen to have known the man who invented barbed wire and who had his abundant reward. Blessings on him! though one is sometimes inclined to add cursings too. It is dangerous stuff to handle. Heavy gloves should always be worn. The flesh is so torn by the ragged barb that the wound is most irritating and hard to heal. When my fence was first erected it was a common thing to find antelope hung up in it, tangled in it, and cut to pieces. Once we found a mustang horse with its head practically cut completely off. The poor brutes had a hard experience in learning the nature of this strange, almost invisible, death-trap stretched across what was before their own free, open and boundless territory. And what frightful wounds some of the ponies would occasionally suffer by perhaps trying to jump over such a fence or even force their way through it; ponies from the far south, equally ignorant with the antelope of the dangers of the innocent-looking slender wire. In another way these fences were sometimes the cause of loss of beast life, as for instance when some of my cattle drifted against the fence during a thunder and rain storm and a dozen of them were killed by one stroke of lightning.

Into this preserve my cattle-breeding stock were put: very few in number to begin with, yet as many as my means afforded. My Company job and salary would soon be a thing of the past and my future must depend entirely on the success of this undertaking. Once before I had boldly, perhaps rashly, taken a lease of a celebrated steer pasture in Carson County, Texas, and gone to Europe to try and float a company, the proposition being to use the pasture, then, and still, the very best in Texas, for wintering yearling steers. No sounder proposition or more promising one could have been put forward. But all my efforts to get the capital needed failed and it was fortunate for me that at the end of one year I succeeded in getting a cancellation of the lease. On first securing the lease the season was well advanced and it became an anxiety to me as to where I should get cattle to put in the pasture, if only enough to pay the year's rent--some 7000 dollars. One man, a canny Scotsman, had been holding and grazing a large herd of 4000 two-year-old steers, all in one straight brand, on the free range just outside. He knew I wanted cattle and I knew he wanted grass, as he could not find a buyer and the season was late. We both played "coon," but I must say I began to feel a bit uncomfortable. At last greatly to my relief and joy, he approached me, and after a few minutes' dickering I had the satisfaction of counting into pasture this immense herd of 4000 cattle. Meantime, I had also been corresponding with another party and very soon afterwards closed a deal with him for some 3700 more two-year-old steers. Thus with 7700 head the pasture was nearly fully stocked, the rent for the first year was assured, and I prepared to go to the Old Country to form the company before mentioned. But before going I found it necessary to throw in a hundred or so old cows to keep the steers quiet. The steers had persisted in walking the fences, travelling in great strings round and round the pasture. They had lots of grass, water and salt, but something else was evidently lacking. Immediately the cows were turned loose all the uneasiness and dissatisfaction ceased. No more fence walking and no more danger (for me) of them breaking out. The family life seemed complete. The suddenness of the effect was very remarkable. This pasture has ever since been used solely for my proposed purpose and every year has been a tremendous success.

First of all a word about my house and home. Built on what may be called the Spanish plan, of adobes (sun-dried bricks), the walls were 2-1/2 feet thick, and there was a courtyard in the centre. Particular attention was paid to the roof, which was first boarded over, then on the boards three inches of mud, and over that sheets of corrugated iron. The whole idea of the adobes and the mud being to secure a cool temperature in summer and warmth in winter. No other materials are so effective.

As explained before, there were no trees or shrubs of any kind within a radius of many miles. So to adorn this country seat I cut and threw into my buggy one day a young shoot of cotton-wood tree, hauled it fifty miles to the ranch, and stuck it in the centre of the court. Water was never too plentiful; so why not make use of the soap-suddy washings which the boys and all of us habitually threw out there? When the tree did grow up, and it thrived amazingly, its shade became the recognized lounging-place. With a few flowering shrubs added the patio assumed quite a pretty aspect. Another feature of the house was that the foundations were laid so deep, and of rock, that skunks could not burrow underneath, which is quite a consideration. Under my winter cottage at the Meadows Ranch in Arizona skunks always denned and lay up during the cold weather, selecting a point immediately under the warm hearthstone. There, as one sat reading over the fire, these delightful animals, within a foot of you, would carry on their family wrangles and in their excitement give evidence of their own nature; but happily the offence was generally a very mild one and evidently not maliciously intended.

Around the house was planted a small orchard and attempts were made at vegetable-growing. But water was too scarce to do the plants justice. Everything must be sacrificed to the cattle. One lesson it taught me, however, and that is that no matter how much water you irrigate with, one good downpour from Nature's fertilizing watering-can is worth more than weeks of irrigation. Rain water has a quality of its own which well or tank water cannot supply. Plants respond to it at once by adopting a cheery, healthy aspect. It had another equally valuable character in that it destroyed the overwhelming bugs. How it destroyed them I don't know: perhaps it drowned them; anyway they disappeared at once.

In my own pasture in New Mexico I for various reasons decided to "breed," instead of simply handle steers. Steers were certainly safer and surer, and the life was an easy one. But there appeared to me greater possibilities in breeding if the cows were handled right and taken proper care of. It will be seen by-and-by that my anticipations were more than justified, so that the success of this little ranch has been a source of pride to me.

The ranch was called "Running Water," because situated on Running Water Draw, a creek that never to my knowledge "ran" except after a very heavy rain. Prairie fires were the greatest danger in this level range country, there being no rivers, canons, or even roads to check their advance. Lightning might set the grass afire; a match carelessly dropped by the cigarette-smoker; a camp fire not properly put out; or any mischievously-inclined individual might set the whole country ablaze. Indeed, the greatest prairie fire I have record of was maliciously started to windward of my ranch by an ill-disposed neighbour (one of the men whose cattle the Scotch Company had closed out and who ever after had a grudge against me) purposely to burn me out. He did not quite succeed, as by hard fighting all night we managed to save half the grass; but the fire extended 130 miles into Texas, burning out a strip from thirty to sixty miles wide. On account of a very high wind blowing that fire jumped my "guard," a term which needs explanation. All round my pasture, on the outside of the fence, for a distance of over forty miles was ploughed a fire-guard thus: two or three ploughed furrows and, 100 feet apart, other two or three ploughed furrows, there being thus a strip of land forty miles long and 100 feet wide. Between these furrows we burnt the grass, an operation that required great care and yet must be done as expeditiously as possible to save time, labour and expense. A certain amount of wind must be blowing so as to insure a clean and rapid burn; but a high gusty wind is most dangerous, as the flames are pretty sure to jump the furrows, enter the pasture, and get away from you. The excitement at such a critical time is of course very great. In such cases it was at first our practice to catch and kill a yearling, split it open and hitch ropes to the hind feet, when two of us mounted men would drag the entire carcass over the line of fire. It was effective but an expensive and cumbrous method. Later I adopted a device called a "drag," composed of iron chains, in the nature of a harrow, covered by a raw hide for smothering purposes. This could be dragged quite rapidly and sometimes had to be used over miles and miles of encroaching fire. The horses might get badly burnt, and in very rank grass where the fierce flames were six to eight feet high it was useless. Sometimes we worked all night, and no doubt it formed a picturesque spectacle and a scene worthy of an artist's brush. Across the centre of the pasture for further safety, as also around the bull and horse pasture, was a similar fire-guard, so that I had in all some fifty-five miles of guard to plough and burn. It is such critical and dangerous, yet necessary, work that I always took care to be present myself and personally boss the operation. Without such a fire-guard one is never free from anxiety. Many other ranchers who were careless in this matter paid dearly for it. These fires were dangerous in other ways. A dear old friend of mine was caught by and burnt to death in one. Another man, a near neighbour, when driving a team of mules, got caught likewise, and very nearly lost his life. He was badly burnt and lost his team.

Hitherto it had been the universal custom of cattlemen to use "grade" bulls, many of them, alas! mere "scrubs" of no breeding at all. No one used pure-bred registered bulls except to raise "grade" bulls with. I determined to use "registered" pure-bred bulls alone, and no others, to raise *steers* with, and was the first man to my knowledge to do so. Neighbours ridiculed the idea, saying that they would not get many calves, that they could not or would not "rustle"--that is, they would not get about with the cows--that they would need nursing and feeding and would not stand the climate. Well, I went east, selected and bought at very reasonable figures the number needed, all very high bred, indeed some of them fashionably so, and took them to the ranch. By the way, bulls were not called bulls in "polite" society: you must call them "males." Very shortly afterwards there was a rise in value of cattle, a strong demand for such bulls, and prices went "out of sight." Thus the bulls that cost me some 100 dollars apiece in a little while were worth 200 or even 300 dollars. The young bulls "rustled" splendidly, and as next spring came along there was much interest felt as to results. To my great delight almost every cow had a calf, and nearly every calf was alike red body and white face, etc. (Hereford). I kept and used these same bulls six or seven seasons; every year got the highest calf-brand or crop amongst all my neighbours; and soon, with prudent culling of the cows, my small herd (some 2000) was the best in the country; and my young steers topped the market, beating even the crack herds that had been established for twenty years and had great reputations.

To give an instance: my principle was to work with little or no borrowed money. Thus my position was such that I did not always *have* to market my steers to pay running expenses; and as I hate trading and dickering, as it is called, my independence gave me a strong position. Well, once when travelling to the ranch I met on the train two "feeders" from the north, who told me they wanted to buy two or three hundred choice two-year-old, high-bred, even, well-coloured and well-shaped steers. Having by chance some photos in my pocket of my steers (as yearlings taken the year before) I produced them. They seemed pleased with them and asked the price, which I told them; but they said no ranch cattle were worth that money and ridiculed the idea of my asking it. "Oh," I said, "it is nothing to me; that is the price of the cattle," but I carefully also told them how to get to my place and invited them to come and see me. Oh, no! they said it was too ridiculous! We travelled on to Amarillo and I at once went out to Running Water. Only two days afterwards, on coming in to dinner, I found my two gentlemen seated on the porch waiting for me. After dinner we saddled up and went out to see the steers. The dealers were evidently surprised and made a long and careful inspection. Evidently they were well pleased, and on returning to the house it was also evident that they were going to adopt the usual tactics of whittling a small piece of wood (a seemingly necessary accompaniment to a trade) and "dickering"; so I again told them my terms, same as before, and hinted that they might take or leave them as they liked. The deal was closed without further ado, some money put up, and next day I started for England, leaving to the foreman the duty and responsibility of delivering the steers at the date specified. These men, like most other operators, were dealing with borrowed money got from commission houses in Kansas City. I learnt afterwards that their Kansas City friends, on hearing of the trade, refused to supply the funds till they had sent a man out specially to see the two-year-old steers that could possibly be worth so much money. He came out, saw them, and reported them to be well worth the price; and they were acknowledged to be the finest small bunch of steers ever shipped out of the south-west country. This was very gratifying indeed.

Another revolution in ranch practice was the keeping up of my bulls in winter-time and not putting them out with the cows till the middle of July. This also met with the ridicule of all the "old-timers"; but it was entirely successful! The calf crop was not only a very large one but the calves were dropped all about the same time, were thus of an even age (an important matter for dealers), and they "came" when their mothers were strong and had lots of milk.

Young cows and heifers having their first calves had to be watched very closely, and we had often to help them in delivery. It may also be mentioned here that the sight of a green, freshly-skinned hide, or a freshly-skinned carcass, will frequently cause cows to "slink" their calves. The smell of blood too creates a tremendous commotion amongst the cattle generally; why, is not quite known.

I also made a practice in early spring of taking up weak or poor cows that looked like needing it, putting them in a separate pasture and feeding them on just two pounds of cotton-seed meal once a day; no hay, only the dry, wild grass in the small pasture. The good effect of even such a pittance of meal was simply astounding. Thereafter I do not think I ever lost a single cow from poverty or weakness. This use of meal on a range ranch was in its way also a novelty. Afterwards it became general and prices of cotton-seed and cotton-seed meal doubled and more.

When a very large number of range cattle, say 2000 or so, required feeding on account of poverty, hay in our country not being obtainable, cotton-seed (whole) would be fed to them by the simple and effective method of loading a large wagon with it, driving it over the pasture, and scattering thinly, not dumping, the seed on to the grass sod. The cattle would soon get so fond of it that they would come running as soon as the wagon appeared and follow it up in a long string, the strongest and greediest closest to the wagon, the poor emaciated, poverty-stricken ones tailing off in the rear. But not one single seed was wasted, everyone being gleaned and picked up in a very short time. It is the best, easiest and most effective way: indeed, the only possible way with such a large number of claimants. And as said before, the recuperating effect of this cotton-seed is simply astonishing. It may be noted, however, that if fed in bulk and to excess the animals will sometimes go blind, which must be guarded against.

In the matter of salt it had become the common practice to use sacked stuff (pulverized) for cattle. There was a strong prejudice against rock salt; so much so that when I decided to buy a carload or two it had to be specially ordered. Another laugh was raised at my proposed use of it. The cattle would get sore tongues, or they would spend so long a time licking it they would have no time to graze, etc., etc. Meantime I had lost some cows by their too quick lapping of the pulverized stuff. Thereafter I never lost one from such a cause and the cattle throve splendidly. Besides, the rock salt was much easier handled and considerably more economical.

My wells were deep, none less than 250 feet, the iron casing 10-inch diameter, the pipe 6-inch or 8-inch, and the mill-wheels 20 feet in diameter; this huge wind power being necessary to pump up from such a depth a sufficiency of water. The water was pumped directly into very large shallow drinking wooden tubs, thence into big reserve earthen tanks (fenced in), and thence again led by pipe to other large drinking-tubs outside and below the tanks, supplied with floating stop-valves. This arrangement, arrived at after much deliberation, worked very well indeed; no water was wasted, and it was always clean; and in very cold weather the cattle always got warm, freshly-pumped well water in the upper tub, an important matter and one reason why my cattle always did so well. But oh, dear! the trouble and work we often had with these wells! Perhaps in zero temperature something would go wrong with the pump valve or the piston leather would wear out, or in a new well the quicksand would work in. Neither myself, foreman nor boy was an expert or had any mechanical knowledge; though continued troubles, much hard work, accompanied by, alas! harder language, was a capital apprenticeship. In bitter cold freezing weather I well remember we once had to pull out the rods and the piping three times in succession before we got the damned thing into shape, and then we did not know what had been the matter. To pull up first 250 feet of heavy rod, disjoint it, and lay it carefully aside; then pull up 250 feet of 6-inch or 8-inch iron piping, in 20-feet lengths, clamp and disjoint it, and put it carefully aside; then to use the sand-bucket to get the sand out of the well if necessary; repair and put into proper shape the valve and cylinder, etc.; then (and these are all parts of one operation), re-lower and connect the 250 feet of heavy piping, the equally long rods, and attach to the mill itself--oh, what anxiety to know if it was going to work or not! On this particular occasion, as stated, we--self, foreman and one boy--actually had to go through this tedious and dangerous performance three times in succession! To pull out the piping great power is needed, and we at first used a capstan made on the ranch and worked by hand. But it was slow work, very slow, and very hard work too; afterwards we used a stout, steady team of horses, with double tackle, and found it to work much more expeditiously. But there was always a great and ever-present danger of the pipe slipping, or a clamp, a bolt, or a hook, or even the rope breaking with disastrous results.

These wells and mills afforded any disgruntled cowhand or "friendly" neighbour a simple and convenient opportunity of "getting even," as a single small nail dropped down a pipe at once clogged the valve and rendered the tedious operation necessary. I had altogether five of such wells.

A little more "brag," if it may be called so, and I shall have done. But it will need some telling, and perhaps credulity on the reader's part. A certain wild plant called "loco" grows profusely in many parts of the Western States; but nowhere more profusely than it did in my pasture. Indeed it looked like this particular spot must have been its place of origin and its stronghold in time of adversity. Certainly, although it was common all over the plains, I never saw in any place such a dense and vigorous growth of it, covering like an alfalfa field solid blocks of hundreds of acres. This is no exaggeration. It had killed a few of our cattle in Arizona and ruined some of our best horses. The Scotch Company lost many hundreds of cattle by it, and also some horses. The plant seems to flourish in cycles of about seven years; that is, though some of it may be present every year it only comes in abundance, overwhelming abundance, once in the period stated. The peculiarity about it, too, is that it grows in the winter months and has flowered and seeded and died down by midsummer. Thus it is the only green and succulent-looking plant to be seen in winter-time on the brown plains. It is very conspicuous and in appearance much resembles clover or alfalfa. Cattle as a rule will avoid it, but for some unknown reason the time comes when you hear the expression the "cattle are eating loco." If so they will continue to eat it, to eat nothing else, till it is all gone; and those eating it will set the example to others, and all that have eaten it will go stark staring mad and the majority of them die. Horses are even more liable to take to it, and are affected exactly in the same way; they go quite crazy, refuse to drink water, cannot be led, and have a dazed, stupid appearance and a tottering gait, till finally they decline and die for want of nourishment. I have seen locoed horses taken up and fed on grain, when some of them recovered and quite got over the habit even of eating the weed; but these were exceptions. Most locoed horses remained too stupid to do anything with and were never of much value. There is one strange fact, however, about them; saddle horses, slightly locoed, just so bad that they cannot be led, and therefore useless as saddlers, do, when hitched up to a wagon or buggy, though never driven before, make splendid work horses. They go like automatons; will trot if allowed till they fall down, and never balk. The worst outlaw horse we ever had, one that had thrown all the great riders of the country and had never been mastered, this absolute devilish beast got a pretty bad dose of the weed; and, to experiment, we hitched him up in a wagon, when lo! he went off like any old steady team horse. This is all very interesting; but that is enough as to its effect on live stock.

At the request of the Department of Agriculture I sent to Washington some specimens of a grub which, when the plant reaches its greatest exuberance and abundance, infests it, eating out its heart and so killing it. It destroys the plant, but alas! generally too late to prevent the seed maturing and falling to earth. The plant itself has been several times carefully examined, its juices tested and experimentally administered to various animals. But no absolutely satisfactory explanation of its effects has been given out; and certainly no antidote or cure of its effects suggested.

Well, in a certain year the seven years' cycle came round; faithfully the loco plant cropped up all over the plains, the seed that had lain dormant for many years germinated and developed everywhere. As winter approached (in October) my fall round-up was due. Calves had to be branded, some old cows sold, and some steers delivered. I had sold nothing that year. On rounding-up the horses many of them showed signs of the weed. The neighbours flocked in and the work began. Only one round-up was made, when the idea seized me that if these cattle were "worked" in the usual way--that is, jammed round, chased about and "milled" for several hours--they would get tired and hungry, and on being turned loose would be inclined to eat whatever was nearest to them--probably the loco plant. It seemed so reasonable a fear, and I was so anxious about the cattle, that I ordered the foreman there and then to turn the herd quietly loose, explained to the neighbours my reasons for doing so, but allowed them to cut out what few cattle they had in the herd: and the year's work was thus at once abandoned. All that winter was a very anxious time. Reports came in from neighbouring ranches that their cattle were dying in hundreds. On driving through their pastures the loco appeared eaten to the ground; all the cattle were after it, and poor, staggering, crazy animals were met on the road without sense enough to get out of your way. By the end of next spring some of my neighbours had few cattle left to round-up. One neighbour, the largest cattle-ranch in the world, owning some 200,000 head, was estimated to have lost at least 20,000. And meantime how were affairs going in my little place? It will seem incredible, but what is here written is absolute truth. The loco was belly high; the self-weaned calves could be seen wading through it; but ne'er a nibbled or eaten plant could be found. I often searched carefully for such dreaded signs but happily always failed: and I did not lose a single cow, calf or steer, nor were any found showing the slightest signs of being affected.

Many reasons were advanced for the miraculous escape of these cattle; people from a hundred miles away came to see and learn the reason. No satisfactory explanation was suggested, and finally they were compelled to accept my own one, and agree that leaving the cattle undisturbed by abandoning the fall round-up was the real solution of the problem. The only work my men did that winter was to keep the fences up and in good shape, and whenever they saw stray cattle in my pasture to turn them out at once, fearing the danger of bad example. Next winter, the loco being still very bad, the same tactics were adopted and only one solitary yearling of mine was affected. So ended the worst loco visitation probably ever experienced in the West; not perhaps that the plant was more abundant than at some other periods, though I think it was, but for some unknown reason the cattle ate it more freely.

The temperature on these plains sometimes went so low as 20 deg. below zero, with wind blowing. There was no natural shelter, literally nothing as big as your hat in the pasture, and several men advised the building of sheds, wind-breaks, etc. But experience told me just the opposite. I had seen cattle (well fed and carefully tended) freeze to death inside sheds and barns. Also I had seen whole bunches of cattle standing shivering behind open sheds and wind-breaks till they practically froze to death or became so emaciated as to eventually die of poverty. If you give cattle shelter they will be always hanging around it. So I built no sheds or anything else. When a blizzard came my cattle had to travel, and the continued travelling backwards and forwards kept the blood in circulation. There were a few cases of horns, feet, ears and mammae frozen off, but I never had a cow frozen to death and never lost any directly from the severity of the weather. More than that, I never fed a pound of hay.

Our name for calves that had lost their mothers, and therefore the nourishment obtained from milk, was "dogies." These dogies were ever afterwards unmistakable in appearance, and remained stunted, "runty" little animals of no value. Yet, if taken up early enough and fed on nourishing diet, they would develop into as large and well-grown cattle as their more fortunate fellows.

My foreman was an ordinary cowboy, but he was a thorough cattleman, had already been in my employ for seven years, and his "little peculiarities" were pretty well known to me. He became desperately jealous of his position (as foreman), resenting interference. It is a good characteristic, this desire for independence, if also accompanied by no fear of responsibility; and on these lines my ranch was run. I allowed him great independence, never interfered so long as he carried out general orders and "ran straight"; but I also put on him full responsibility. More than that, I allowed him to run his own small bunch of cattle, some hundred head, in my pasture, and gave him the use of my bulls; his grass, salt and water cost him nothing. This was a very unusual policy to adopt. But the idea was that it would thus be as much his interest as mine to see the fences kept up and in good repair, to see that the windmills and wells were kept in order, that the cattle had salt, were not stolen, etc., and prairie fires guarded against. Well, it all turned out right. My presence at the ranch during a year would not perhaps amount to a month of days; I could live in Denver, San Francisco or Mexico, and only come to the place at round-ups and branding-times. I do not think that a calf was ever stolen from me. The fact was I knew cattle in general and my own cattle in particular so well (and he knew it) that he had no opportunity, and perhaps was afraid to take advantage of me.

It must be here mentioned that on selling out, and in tallying my cattle over to the buyer, the count was disappointingly short; not nearly so short as the Scotch Company's cattle, it is true, but still, considering that my cattle were inside a good fence, were well looked after, the huge calf crop and apparently small death loss, there was a shortage. Then there is no wonder at the greater shortage of the Company's cattle, where almost no care could be taken of them, where the calf tallies were in the hands of, and returned by, the foremen of other outfits, where the range was overstocked, the boggy rivers a death-trap, where wolves and thieves had free range, and where blackleg, mismothering of calves and loco made a big hole in the number of yearlings. In my pasture were also wolves and blackleg; and the loss in calves by these, difficult to detect, is invariably greater than suspected.

Only one case of cattle-thieving occurred at my own ranch and I lost nothing by it. Two men stopped in for supper one day; they were strangers, but of course received every attention. They rode on afterwards, coolly picked up some thirty head of my cattle, drove them all night into Texas and sold them to a farmer there. Of course they were not missed out of so many cattle; but someone in Texas had seen them at their new home, noticed my brand and sent word to me. On going after them I found they had been sold to an innocent man who had paid cash for them and taken no bill of sale. It was not a pleasant duty to demand the cattle back from such a man, but he ought to have known better.

Some rustlers in Arizona once detached from a train at a small station a couple of carloads of beef cattle, ran them back down the track to the corral, there unloaded the cattle and drove them off. This very smart trick of course was done during the night and while the crew were at supper.

For all these reasons it will be seen why my small ranch was such a success and such a profitable and money-making institution. But alas! it was to be short-lived! As explained before, I was paying no rent and my fences were illegal. "Kind" friends, and I had lots of them, reported the fences to Washington; a special agent was sent out to inspect, ordered the fence down and went away again. I disregarded the order. To take the fence down meant my getting out of the business or the ruin of the herd. Next year another agent came out, said my fence was an enclosure and must come down. Seeing still some daylight I took down some few miles of it, so that it could not be defined as an enclosure, but only a drift-fence. During the winter, however, I could not resist closing the gap again. Next season once more appeared a Government agent, who in a rage ordered the fence down under pains and penalties which could not well be longer disregarded. Cattle were up in price; a neighbour had long been anxious to buy me out; he was somewhat of a "smart Alick" and thought *he* could keep the fence up; he knew all the circumstances; so I went over and saw him, made a proposition, and in a few minutes the ranch, cattle, fences and mills were his. Poor man! in six months his fence was down and the cattle scattered all over the country. He eventually lost heavily by the deal; but being a man of substance I got my money all right. So closed my cattle-ranching experiences some eight years ago (1902).

It may be noted that experience showed that polled black bulls were no good for ranch purposes. They get few calves, are lazy, and have not the "rustling" spirit. Durhams or Shorthorns also compared poorly in these respects with Herefords, and besides are not nearly so hardy. The white face is therefore king of the range. And bulls with red rings round the eyes by preference, as they can stand the bright glare of these hot, dry countries better. It used to be my keen delight to attend the annual cattle shows and auction sales of pure-bred bulls, and I would feel their hides and criticize their points till I almost began to imagine myself as competent as the ring judges.

The ranch was in the heart of the great buffalo range. (Indeed the Comanche Indians, and even some white men, used to believe firmly that the buffaloes each spring came up out of the ground like ants somewhere on these Staked Plains, and from thence made their annual pilgrimage north.) It seems these animals were not loco eaters.

On my first coming to New Mexico there were still some buffaloes on the plain, the last remnant of the uncountable, inconceivable numbers that not long before had swarmed over the country. Even when the first railroads were built trains were sometimes held up for hours to let the herds pass. As late as 1871 Colonel Dodge relates that he rode for twenty-five miles directly through an immense herd, the whole country around him and in view being like a solid mass of buffaloes, all moving north. In fact, during these years the migrating herd was declared to have a front of thirty to forty miles wide, while the length or depth was unknown. An old buffalo hunter loves nothing better than to talk of the wonderful old times. One of the oldest living ranchmen still has a private herd near Amarillo and has made many experiments in breeding the bulls to domestic Galloway cows. The progeny, which he calls cattalo, make excellent beef, and he gets a very big price for the hides as robes.

CHAPTER VIII
ODDS AND ENDS

The "Staked Plains"--High Winds--Lobo Wolves--Branding--Cows-
-Black   Jack--Lightning and Hail--Classing Cattle--Conventions-
-"Cutting"   versus Polo--Bull-Fight--Prize-Fights--River and Sea
Fishing--Sharks.

More odds and ends! and more apologies for the disconnected character of this chapter. It must be remembered that these notes are only jotted down as they have occurred to me. Of their irrelativeness one to another I am quite conscious, but the art of bringing them together in more proper order is beyond my capacity. Possibly it might not be advisable anyway. In my pasture of some 100,000 acres there was not a tree, a bush, or a shrub, or object of any nature bigger than a jack-rabbit; yet no sight was so gladsome to the eyes, no scenery (save the mark!) so beautiful as the range when clothed in green, the grass heading out, the lakes filled with water and the cattle fat, sleek and contented. Yet in after years, when passing through this same country by the newly-built railway in winter-time, it came as a wonder to me how one could have possibly passed so many years of his life in such a dreary, desolate, uninteresting-looking region. To-day the whole district, even my own old and familiar ranch, is desecrated (in the cattleman's eyes) by little nesters' (settlers) cottages, and fences so thick and close together as to resemble a Boer entanglement. I had done a bit of farming and some years raised good crops of Milo maize, Kafir corn, sorghum, rye, and even Indian corn. But severe droughts come on, when, as a nester once told me, for two years nothing was raised, not even umbrellas!

These plains are, it may be safely said, the windiest place on earth, especially in early spring, when the measured velocity sometimes shows eighty miles per hour. When the big circular tumble weeds are bounding over the plains then is the time to look out for prairie fires; and woe betide the man caught in a blizzard in these lonely regions.

Once when driving from a certain ranch to another, a distance of fifty miles, my directions were to "follow the main road." Fifty miles was no great distance and my team was a good one. I knew there were no houses between the two points. After driving what long experience told me was more than fifty miles, and still no ranch, I became a bit anxious; but there was nothing for it but to keep going. Black clouds in the north warned me of danger. I pushed the team along till they were wet with sweat; some snow fell; it grew dark as night; and a regular blizzard set in and I was in despair. I had a good bed in the buggy, so would myself probably have got through the night all right, but my horses were bound to freeze to death if staked out or tied up. As a last resource I threw the reins down and left it to the team to go wherever they pleased. For some time they kept on the road, but soon the jolting told me that they had left it and we began to go down a hill; in a little while great was my joy to see a light and to find ourselves soon in the hospitable shelter of a Mexican sheep-herder's hut. The Mexican unhitched the team and put them in a warm shed. For myself, he soon had hot coffee and tortillas on the table. I never felt so thankful in my life for such accommodation and such humble fare. The horses had never been in that part of the country before, that I knew; it was pitch dark, and yet they must have known in some mysterious way that in that direction was shelter and safety, as when I threw the lines down they even then continued to face the storm.

It may be noted here that buffaloes always face the storm and travel against it; cattle and horses never.

Before entirely leaving the cattle business a few more notes may be of interest.

Plagues of grasshoppers and locusts sometimes did awful damage to the range.

When visiting at a neighbour's one must not dismount till invited to do so; also in saluting anyone the gloves must be removed before shaking hands. This is cowboy etiquette and must be duly regarded.

At public or semi-private dances there is always a master of ceremonies, who is also prompter and calls out all the movements. He will announce a "quardreele," or maybe a "shorteesche," and keeps the company going with his "Get your partners!" "Balance all!" "Swing your partners!" "Hands across!" "How do you do?" and "How are you?" "Swing somewhere," and "Don't forget the bronco-buster," etc. etc., as someone has described it. The Mexicans are always most graceful dancers; cowboys, with their enormously high heels, and probably spurs, are a bit clumsy. At purely Mexican dances (Bailies) the two sexes do not speak, each retiring at the end of a dance to its own side of the room.

Most cowboys have the peculiar faculty of "humming," produced by shaping the mouth and tongue in a certain way. The "hum" can be made to exactly represent the bagpipes; no one else did I ever hear do it but cowpunchers. I have tried for hours but never quite succeeded in the art.

Besides coyotes, which are everywhere common, the plains were infested by lobo wolves, a very large and powerful species; they denned in the breaks of the plains and it was then easiest to destroy them. They did such enormous damage amongst cattle that a reward of as high as thirty dollars per scalp was frequently offered for them, something less for the pups. The finding of a nest with a litter of perhaps six to eight young ones meant considerable money to the scalp-hunter. The wolves were plentiful and hunted in packs; and I have seen the interesting sight of a small bunch of mixed cattle rounded up and surrounded by a dozen of them, sitting coolly on their haunches till some unwary yearling left the protecting horns of its elders. Every time, when riding the range, that we spotted a lobo ropes were down at once and a more or less long chase ensued, the result depending much whether Mr Wolf had dined lately or not. But they were more addicted to horse and donkey flesh if obtainable. For purposes of poisoning them I used to buy donkeys at a dollar apiece and cut them up for bait. With hounds they gave good sport in a suitable country. But it is expensive work, as many dogs get killed, and no dog of any breed, unless maybe the greyhound, can or will singly and twice tackle a lobo wolf.

In the springtime, when the calves are dropping pretty thick, it is exceedingly interesting to note the protective habits of the mother cows. For instance, when riding you will frequently come on a two or three days' old baby snugly hidden in a bunch of long grass while the mother has gone to water. When calves get a little older you may find at mid-day, out on the prairie, some mile or two from water, a bunch of maybe forty calves. Their mammies have gone to drink; but not all of them! No, never all of them at the same time. One cow is always left to guard the helpless calves, and carries out her trust faithfully until relieved. This was and is still a complete mystery to me. Does this individual cow select and appoint herself to the office; or is she balloted for, or how otherwise is the selection made?

This might be another picture subject--the gallant cow on the defensive, even threatening and aggressive, and the many small helpless calves gathering hastily around her for protection. Her! The self-appointed mother of the brood.

When branding calves, suppose you have 400 cows and calves in the corral. First all calves are separated into a smaller pen. Then the branding begins. But what an uproar of bellows and "baas" takes place! My calves were all so very like one another in colour and markings that one was hardly distinguishable from another. The mothers can only recognize their hopeful offspring by their scent and by their "baa," although amongst 400 it must be rather a nice art to do so--400 different and distinct scents and 400 differently-pitched baas.

Among these notes I should not forget to mention a brush plant that grows on the southern plains. It is well named the "wait-a-bit" thorn. Its hooks or claws are sharper than a cat's, very strong and recurve on the stems: so that a man afoot cannot possibly advance through it, and even on a horse it will tear the trousers off you in a very few minutes. Is the name not appropriate?

Nothing so far has been said on the subject of "hold-ups." Railway train hold-ups were a frequent occurrence, and were only undertaken by the most desperate of men. One celebrated gang, headed by the famous outlaw, Black Jack, operated mostly on a railway to the north of us and another railway to the south, the distance between being about 400 miles. Their line of travel between these two points was through Fort Sumner; and in our immediate neighbourhood they sometimes rested for a week or two, hiding out as it were, resting horses and laying plans. No doubt they cost us some calves for beef, though they were not the worst offenders. What annoyed me most was that Black Jack himself, when evading pursuit, raided my horse pasture one night, caught up the very best horse I ever owned, rode him fifty miles, and cut his throat.

In New Mexico, where at first it seemed everybody's hand was against me, I was gratified to find that I had got a reputation as a fist-fighter, and as I never prac-

tised boxing in my life, never had the gloves on, never had a very serious fist fight
with anyone, the idea of having such a reputation was too funny; but why should
one voluntarily repudiate it? It was useful. The men had also somehow heard that I
could hold a six-shooter pretty straight. Such a reputation was even more useful. I
was not surprised therefore that a plan should be hatched to test my powers in that
line. It came at the round-up dinner-hour on the Company's range (New Mexico).
A small piece of board was nailed to a fence post and the boys began shooting at it.
In a casual way someone asked me to try my hand. Knowing how much depended
on it I got out my faithful old 45 deg. six-shooter that I had carried for fifteen years,
and taking quick aim, as much to my own surprise as to others', actually hit the
centre of the mark! It was an extraordinarily good shot (could not do it again perhaps in twenty trials) but it saved my reputation. Of course no pressure could have
persuaded me to fire again. That reminds me of another such occasion.

Once when camped alone on the Reservation in Arizona, a party of officers
from Camp Apache turned up. They had a bite to eat with me and the subject of
shooting came up. Someone stuck an empty can in a tree at a considerable distance
from us and they began shooting at it with carbines. When my turn came I pulled
out the old 45 deg. pistol and by lucky chance knocked the bottom out at the first
shot. My visitors were amazed that a six-shooter had such power and could be used
with such accuracy at that distance. In this case it was also a lucky shot; but constant practice at rabbits, prairie dogs and targets had made me fairly proficient. In
New Mexico I had a cowboy working for me who was a perfect marvel, a "born"
marksman such as now and then appears in the West. With a carbine he could keep
a tin can rolling along the ground by hitting, never the can, but just immediately
behind and under it with the greatest accuracy. If one tossed nickel pieces (size of
a shilling) in succession in front of him he would hit almost without fail every one
of them with his carbine--a bullet not shot! He left me to give exhibition shooting
at the Chicago Exposition.

On my ranch, at Running Water Draw, was unearthed during damming operations, a vast quantity of bones of prehistoric age; which calls for the remark that not
only the horse but also the camel was at one time indigenous to North America.

Nothing has been said yet about hail or lightning storms. Some of the latter
were indescribably grand, when at night the whole firmament would be absolutely

ablaze with flashes, sheets and waves so continuous as to be without interval. Once when lying on my bed on the open prairie such a storm came on. It opened with loud thunder and some brilliant flashes, then the rain came down and deluged us, the water running two inches deep over the grass; and when the rain ceased the wonderful electric storm as described continued for an hour longer. The danger was over; but the sight was awe-inspiring in the extreme. Night-herding too during such a storm was a strange experience. No difficulty to see the cattle; the whole herd stood with tails to the wind; the men lined out in front, each well covered by his oilskin slicker, and his horse's tail likewise turned to the storm; the whole outfit in review order so to speak, the sole object of the riders being to prevent the cattle from "drifting." This book contains no fiction or exaggeration; yet it will be hardly believed when I state that hail actually riddled the corrugated iron roof of my ranch house--new iron, not old or rusty stuff. The roof was afterwards absolutely useless as a protection against rain.

Mirages in the hot dry weather were a daily occurrence. We did not see imaginary castles and cities turned upside down and all that sort of thing, but apparent lakes of water were often seen, so deceptive as to puzzle even the oldest plainsman. Cattle appeared as big as houses and mounted men as tall as church steeples.

In all the vicious little cow-towns scattered about the country, whose attractions were gambling and "tarantula juice," there was always to be found a Jew trader running the chief and probably only store in the place. I have known such a man arrive in the country with a pack on his back who in comparatively few years would own half the county.

What a remarkable people the Jews are! We find them all over the world (barring Scotland) successful in almost everything they undertake, a prolific race, and good citizens, yet carrying with them in very many cases the characteristics of selfishness, greed and ostentation.

Something should be said about "classing" cattle. "Classing" means separating or counting the steers or she cattle of a herd into their ages as yearlings, "twos," "threes," etc. It used to be done in old days by simply stringing the herd out on the open plain and calling out and counting each animal as it passed a certain point. But later it became the custom to corral the herd and run them through a chute, where each individual could be carefully inspected and its age agreed on by both parties. Even that might not prove quite satisfactory, as will be shown in the following instance. I had sold to a certain gentleman (a Scotchman again), manager for two large cattle companies, a string of some 1000 steers, one, two and three years old. I drove them to his ranch, some 300 miles, and we began classing them on the prairie, cutting each class separately. It is difficult in many cases to judge a range steer's age. Generally it is or should be a case of give-and-take. But my gentleman was not satisfied and expressed his dissatisfaction in not very polite language. So to satisfy him I agreed to put them through the chute and "tooth" them, the teeth being an infallible test (or at least the accepted test) of an animal's age. To my surprise this man, the confident, trusted manager of long years' experience, could not tell a yearling from a "two" or a "two" from a "three," but sat on the fence and cussed, and allowed his foreman to do the classing for him.

The Texas Cattlemen's Annual Convention was a most important event in our lives. It was held sometimes in El Paso, sometimes in San Antonio, but oftenest in Fort Worth, and was attended by ranchmen from all over the State, as well as by many from New Mexico, and by buyers from Wyoming, Montana, Nebraska, Kansas and elsewhere. Being held early in spring the sales then made generally set the prices for the year. Much dickering was gone through and many deals made, some of enormous extent. Individual sales of 2000, 5000 or even 10,000 steers were effected, and individual purchases of numbers up to 20,000 head; even whole herds of 30,000 to 50,000 cattle were sometimes disposed of. It was a meeting where old friends and comrades, cattle kings and cowboys, their wives, children and sweethearts, met and had a glorious old time. It brought an immense amount of money into the place, and hence the strenuous efforts made by different towns (the saloons) "to get the Convention."

Among the celebrities to be met there might be Buffalo Jones, a typical plainsman of the type of Buffalo Bill (Cody). Jones some years ago went far north to secure some young musk oxen. None had ever before been captured. He and his men endured great hardships and privations, but finally, by roping, secured about a dozen yearlings. The Indians swore that he should not take them out of their territory. On returning he had got as far as the very edge of the Indian country and was a very proud and well-pleased man. But that last fatal morning he woke up to find all the animals with their throats cut. Only last year Jones, with two New Mexican cowboys and a skilled photographer, formed the daring and apparently mad plan of going to Africa and roping and so capturing any wild animal they might come across, barring, of course, the elephant. His object was to secure for show purposes cinematograph pictures. He took some New Mexican cow-ponies out with him, and he and his men succeeded in all they undertook to do, capturing not only the less dangerous animals, such as antelope, buck and giraffe, but also a lioness and a rhinoceros, surely a very notable feat.

Amarillo in the Panhandle was then purely a cattleman's town. It was a great shipping point--at one time the greatest in the world--and was becoming a railroad centre. I was there a good deal, and for amusement during the slack season went to work to fix up a polo ground. No one in the town had ever even seen the game played, so the work and expense all fell on myself. I was lucky to find a capital piece of ground close to the town, absolutely level and well grassed. After measuring and laying off, with a plough I ran furrows for boundary lines, stuck in the goalposts, filled up the dog-holes, etc., and there we were. At first only three or four men came forward, out of mere curiosity perhaps. After expounding the game and the rules, etc., as well as possible we started in to play. The game soon "caught on," and in a little while a number more joined, nearly all cattlemen and cowpunchers. They became keen and enthusiastic, too keen sometimes, for in their excitement they disregarded the rules. The horses, being cow-ponies, were of course as keen and as green as the players, and the game became a most dangerous one to take part in. Still we kept on, no one was very badly hurt, and we had lots of glorious gallops--fast games in fact.

The word "polo" is derived from Tibetan pulu, meaning a knot of willow wood. In Cachar, and also at Amarillo, we used bamboo-root balls. The game originated in Persia, passed to Tibet, and thence to the Munipoories, and from the Munipoories the English learnt it. The first polo club ever organized was the Cachar Kangjai Club, founded in 1863. It may be remarked here that, hard as the riding is in polo, in my opinion it does not demand nearly such good riding as does the "cutting" of young steers. In polo your own eye is on the ball, and when another player or yourself hits it you know where to look for it, and rule your horse accordingly. In "cutting," on the other hand, your horse, if a good one, does nearly all the work; just show it the animal you want to take out and he will keep his eye on it and get it out of the herd without much guidance. But there is this great difference: you never can tell what a steer is going to do! You may be racing or "jumping" him out of the herd when he will suddenly flash round before you have time to think and break back again. Herein your horse is quicker than yourself, knowing apparently instinctively the intention of the rollicky youngster, so that both steer and your mount have wheeled before you are prepared for it. You must therefore try to be always prepared, sit very tight, and profit by past experiences. It is very hard work and, as said before, needs better horsemanship than polo. To watch, or better still to ride, a first-class cutting horse is a treat indeed.

During these last few years of ranch life my leisure gave me time to make odd excursions here and there. Good shooting was to be had near Amarillo--any amount of bobwhite quail, quantities of prairie-chickens, plovers, etc. And, by-the-bye, at Fort Sumner I had all to myself the finest kind of sport. There was a broad avenue of large cotton-wood trees some miles in length. In the evening the doves, excellent eating, and, perhaps for that reason, tremendously fast fliers, would flash by in twos or threes up or down this avenue, going at railroad speed. But my pleasure was marred by having no companion to share the sport.

Then I made many trips to the Rocky Mountains to fish for rainbow trout in such noble streams as the Rio Grande del Norte, the Gunnison, the Platte and others. In the early days these rivers were almost virgin streams, hotching with trout of all sizes up to twelve and even fifteen pounds. The monsters could seldom be tempted except with spoon or live bait, but trout up to six or seven pounds were common prizes. Out of a small, a ridiculously small, tributary of the Gunnison River I one day took more fish than I could carry home, each two to three pounds in weight. But that was murdering--mere massacre and not sport.

During a cattle convention held at El Paso I first attended a bull-fight in Juarez and I have since seen others in the city of Mexico and elsewhere. The killing of the poor blindfolded horses is a loathsome, disgusting sight, and so affected me that I almost prayed that the gallant, handsome matadors would be killed. Indeed, at Mexico City, I afterwards saw Bombita, a celebrated Spanish matador, tossed and gored to death. The true ring-bull of fighting breed is a splendid animal; when enraged he does not seem to suffer much from the insertion of banderillas, etc., and his death stab is generally instantaneously fatal. Certainly the enthusiasm of the ring, the presence of Mexican belles and their cavalleros, the picturesqueness and novelty of the whole show are worth experiencing.

It should be remembered that the red cloth waved in front of him is the main cause of Toro's irritation. Why it should so irritate him we don't know. When a picador and his horse are down they are absolutely at the mercy of the bull; and the onlooker naturally thinks that he will proceed to gore man and horse till they are absolutely destroyed. But the cloth being at once flaunted near him he immediately attacks it instead and is thus decoyed to another part of the ring. Thus, too, the apparent danger to the swordsman who delivers the *coup de grace* is not really very great if he show the necessary agility and watchfulness. When a bull charges he charges not his real enemy, but that exasperating red cloth; and the man has only to step a little to the side, but *still hold the cloth in front* of the bull, to escape all danger. Without this protecting cloth no matador would dare to enter the ring. The banderilleros, too, thus escape danger because they do their work while the bull's whole attention is on the red cloth operated by another man in front. The man I saw gored, tossed and killed must have made some little miscalculation, or been careless, and stood not quite out of the bull's way, so that the terrible sharp horns caught him, as one may say, *by mistake*.

The Mexicans, too, like my coolies in India, were great cock-fighters. It is a national sport and also a cruel one.

Matadors are paid princely sums. The most efficient, the great stars, come from Spain. Many of them are extremely handsome men and their costume a handsome and picturesque one. As a mark of their profession they wear a small pigtail, not artificial but of their own growing hair. I travelled with one once but did not know it till he removed his hat.

Denver and San Francisco were great centres of prize-fighting. In both places I saw many of the great ring men of the day, in fact never missed an opportunity of attending such meetings. It was mostly, however, "goes" between the "coming" men, such as Jim Corbett and other aspirants. A real champion fight between heavy-weights I was never lucky enough to witness.

Base-ball games always appealed to me, and to witness a first-class match only a very great distance would prevent my attendance. To appreciate the game one must thoroughly understand its thousand fine points. It absorbs the onlooker's interest as no other game can do. Every player must be constantly on the alert and must act on his own judgment. The winning or losing of the match may at any moment lie with him. The game only lasts some two hours; but for the onlookers every moment of these two hours is pregnant with interest and probably intense excitement. Here is no sleeping and dozing on the stands for hours at a time as witnessed at popular cricket matches. Time is too valuable in America for that, and men's brains are too restless. At a ball-game the sight of a man slumbering on the benches is inconceivable.

Sea-fishing also attracted me very much. On the California coast, around Catalina and other islands, great sport is to be had among the yellow-tails, running up to 50 lbs. weight. They are a truly game fish and put up a capital fight. Jew-fish up to 400 lbs. are frequently caught with rod and line, but are distinctly not a game fish. Albacores can be taken in boat-loads; they are game enough but really too common. The tuna is *par excellence* the game fish of the coast. At one time you might reasonably expect to get a fish (nothing under 100 lbs. counted), but lately, and while I was there, a capture was so rare as to make the game not worth the candle. A steam or motor launch is needed and that costs money. I hired such a boat once or twice; but the experience of some friends who had fished every day for two months and not got one single blessed tuna damped my ambition. Tunas there run up to 300 lbs., big enough, and yet tiny compared with the monsters of the Mediterranean, the Morocco coast and the Japanese seas; there they run up to 2000 lbs. The tuna is called the "leaping" tuna because he plays and hunts his prey on the surface of the water; but he never "leaps" as does the tarpon. Once hooked he goes off to sea and will tow your boat maybe fifteen miles; that is to say, he partly tows the boat, but the heavy motor launch must also use its power to keep up or the line will at once be snapped. The tuna belongs to the mackerel family, is built like a white-head torpedo, and for gameness, speed and endurance is hard to beat. Only the pala of the South Pacific Seas, also a mackerel, may, according to Louis Becke, be his rival. Becke indeed claims it to be the gamest of all fish. But its manoeuvres are different from a tuna's and similar to those of the tarpon. What is finer sport, I think, and perhaps not quite so killing to the angler, is tarpon-fishing. Most of our ambitious tarpon fishers go to Florida, where each fish captured will probably cost you some fifty dollars. My tarpon ground was at Aransas Pass, on the Gulf Coast of Texas. There in September the fish seem to congregate preparatory to their migration south. I have seen them there in bunches of fifty to seventy, swimming about in shallow, clear water, their great dorsal fins sticking out, for all the world like a lot of sharks. My first experience on approaching in a small row boat such an accumulation of fish muscle, grit and power will never be forgotten. It was one of *the* events of my chequered life. The boatman assured me I should get a "strike" of a certainty as soon as the bait was towed within sight of them. My state of excitement was so great that really all nerve force was gone. My muscles, instead of being tense and strong, seemed to be relaxed and feeble; my whole body was in a tremble. To see these monster fish of 150 to 200 lbs. swimming near by, and to know that next moment a tremendous rush and fight would begin, was to the novice almost a painful sensation. Not quite understanding the mechanism of the powerful reel and breaks, and being warned that thumbs or fingers had sometimes been almost torn off the hand, I grasped the rod very gingerly. But I need not say what my first fish or any particular fish did or what happened. I will only say that I got all I wanted--enough to wear me out physically till quite ready to be gaffed myself. It is tremendously hard work. To rest myself and vary the sport I would leave the tarpon and tackle the red-fish, an equally game and fighting fish, but much smaller, scaling about 15 to 20 lbs. There was a shoal of them visible, or at least a bunch of about 100, swimming right on the edge of the big breaking surf. Like the tarpon they thus keep close company on account of the sharks (supposition). It was dangerous and difficult to get the boat near enough to them; but when you did succeed there was invariably a rush for your bait and a game fight to follow. They are splendid chaps. Then I would return to the tarpon and have another battle royal; and so it went on. But sometimes you would hook a jack fish (game, and up to 25 lbs.), and sometimes get into a shark of very big proportions. Indeed, the sharks are a nuisance, and will sometimes cut your tarpon in two close to your boat, and they eagerly await the time when you land your fish and unhook him to turn him loose.

Another noble fish, of which I was lucky enough to get several, was the king-fish, long, pike-shaped and silvery, a most beautiful creature, and probably the fastest fish that swims. I had not realized just how quick any fish could swim till I hooked one of these. He acts much as the tarpon does. But I have not yet told how the latter, the king of the herring race, does act. On being hooked he makes a powerful rush for a hundred yards or so; then he springs straight up high out of the water, as much as six to ten feet, shakes his head exactly as a terrier does with a rat, falls back to make another rush and another noble spring. He will make many springs before you dare take liberties and approach the landing shore. But the peculiarity of this fish is that his runs are not all in one direction. His second run may take quite a different line; and at any time he may run and spring into or over your boat. When two anglers have fish on at the same time, and in close neighbourhood, the excitement and fun are great. The tarpon's whole mouth, palate and jaws have not a suspicion of muscle or cartilage about them; all is solid bone, with only a few angles and corners where it is possible for the hook to take good hold. Unless the hook finds such a fold in the bones you are pretty sure to lose your fish--three out of four times. Probably by letting him gorge the bait you will get him all right, but it would entail killing him to get the hook out. In winter the tarpons go south, and perhaps the best place to fish them is at Tempico in Mexico. But let me strongly recommend Aransas Pass in September. There is good quail-shooting, rabbits, and thousands of water-fowl of every description; also a very fair little hotel where I happened to be almost the only visitor. At Catalina Islands, by the way, whose climate is absolutely delightful, where there are good hotels, and where the visitors pass the whole day in the water or on land in their bathing-suits, one can hire glass-bottom boats, whereby to view the wonderful and exquisitely beautiful flora of the sea, and watch the movements of the many brilliantly-coloured fish and other creatures that inhabit it. The extraordinary clearness of the water there is particularly favourable for the inspection of these fairy bowers. One day I determined to try for a Jew-fish, just to see how such a huge, ungainly monster would act. Anchoring, we threw the bait over, and in a short time I pulled in a rock cod of nearly 7 lbs. weight. My boatman coolly threw the still hooked fish overboard again, telling me it would be excellent bait for the big ones we were after. Well, I did not get the larger fish; but the sight on looking overboard into the depths was so astonishing as to be an ample reward for any other disappointment. On the surface was a dense shoal of small mullet or other fish; below them, six or eight feet, another shoal of an entirely different kind; below these another shoal of another kind, and so on as far down as the eye could penetrate. It was a most marvellous sight indeed, and showed what a teeming life these waters maintain. It seemed that a large fish had only to lie still with its huge mouth open, and close it every now and then when he felt hungry, to get a dinner or a luncheon fit for any fishy alderman. It must be a fine field for the naturalist, the ichthyologist, probably as fine as that round Bermudas' coral shores, as illustrated by the new aquarium at Hamilton. But I can hardly think that the fish of any other climate can compare for brilliancy of colouring and fantastic variety of shape with those captured on the Hawaiian coast and well displayed in the aquarium at Honolulu.

I must not forget to mention that at Aransas Pass one may sometimes see very large whip or sting-rays. They may easily be harpooned, but the wonderful stories told me of their huge size (I really dare not give the dimensions), their power and ferocity, quite scared me off trying conclusions with them. There one may also capture blue-fish, white-fish, sheepheads and pompanos; all delicious, the pompanos being the most highly-prized and esteemed, and most expensive, of America's many fine table fishes. Order a pompano the first opportunity.

Having already mentioned sharks, it may be stated here that one captured in a net on the California coast four years ago was authoritatively claimed to be the largest ever taken, yet his length was only some 36 feet; although it is true that the *Challenger* Expedition dredged up shark teeth so large that it was judged that the owner must have been 80 to 90 feet long. The Greynurse shark of the South Seas is the most dreaded of all its tribe; it fears nothing but the Killer, a savage little whale which will attack and whip any shark living, and will not hesitate to tackle even a sperm whale. Shark stories are common and every traveller has many horrible ones to recount. Yet the greatest and best authorities assert that sharks are mere scavengers (as they are, and most useful ones) and will never attack an active man, or any man, unless he be in extremities--that is, dead, wounded or disabled; though, as among tigers, there probably are some man-eaters. A large still-standing reward has been offered for a fully-certified case of a shark voluntarily attacking a man, other than exceptions as above noted, and that reward has not yet been claimed. Whenever I hear a thrilling shark story I ask if the teller is prepared to swear to having himself witnessed the event; invariably the experience is passed on to someone else and the responsibility for the tale is laid on other shoulders. On a quite recent voyage a talkative passenger confidently stated having seen a shark 70 feet long. I ventured to measure out that distance on the ship's deck, and asked him and his credulous listeners to regard and consider it. It gained me an enemy for life.

One of the most famous and historical sharks was San Jose Joe, who haunted the harbour of Corinto, a small coast town in Salvador. Every ship that entered the harbour was sure to have some bloodthirsty fiend on board to empty his cartridges into this unfortunate creature. His carcass was reckoned to be as full of lead as a careful housewife's pin-cushion of pins. But all this battering had no effect on him. Finally, and after my own visit to that chief of all yellow-fever-stricken dens, a British gun-boat put a shell into Joe and blew him into smithereens. In many shark-infested waters, such as around Ocean Island, the natives swim fearlessly among them. This ocean island, by the way, is probably the most intrinsically valuable spot of land on earth, consisting of a solid mass of coral and phosphate. "Pelorus Jack," who gave so much interest to the Cook Channel in New Zealand, was not a shark.

CHAPTER IX
IN AMARILLO

Purchase of Lots--Building--Boosting a Town.

Enough of odds and ends. To return to purely personal affairs. After selling the cattle and ranch the question at once came up--What now? I had enough to live on, but not enough to allow me to live quite as I wished, though never ambitious of great wealth. What had been looked forward to for many years was to have means enough to permit me to travel over the world; and at the same time to have my small capital invested in such a way as would secure not only as big a per cent. interest as possible, with due security, but also a large probability of unearned increment, so to speak; and above all to require little personal attention. Dozens of schemes presented themselves, many with most rosy outlooks. I was several times on the very verge of decision, and how easily and differently one's whole future may be affected! Perhaps by now a millionaire!--perhaps a pauper! At one time I was on the point of buying a cotton plantation in the South. The only obstacle was the shortage of convict labour! A convict negro *must* work; the free negro won't. Finally I bought some city lots in the town of Amarillo--the most valuable lots I could find, right at the city's pulse, the centre of business; in my judgment they would in all probability always be at the centre, and that as the city grew so would their value grow, and thus the unearned increment would be secured. I bought these lots by sheer pressure; the owner did not want to sell, but I made him name his own price, and closed the deal, to his astonishment. It was a record price and secured me some ridicule. But the funniest part has to come. In a little while I became dissatisfied with my deal, and actually approached the seller and asked him if he would cancel it. He too had regretted parting with the property, and to my relief assented. Once more I spent nearly a year ranging about the whole western country, looking into different propositions, and again I came back to Amarillo, again was impressed with the desirability of the same lots, and actually demanded of the still more astonished owner if he would sell them to me. No! no! he did not want to part with them; and I knew he spoke the truth. Again I forced him, and so hard that at last he put on what he considered a prohibitory price, a much higher one than before asked, but I snapped him up at once. The news soon got all over town, it could not be kept quiet. Once more the supposed knowing ones and "cute" business men eyed me askance, and no doubt thought me a fool, or worse. Only one man approved of my action, but I valued his opinion more than that of all the rest. This deal again made a stir amongst the Real Estate offices, and lot values went soaring; and when I had erected a handsome business block on the property a regular "boom" set in. It gave the little town a lift and the people confidence. One man was good enough to tell me that I had more "nerve" than anyone he had ever met. Did he mean rashness? Well, my nerve simply came from realizing what a fine outlook lay before the town. It seemed to me to be bound to be a great distributing centre, also a railroad centre; that the illimitable acreage of plains-lands was bound in time to be settled on, and that thus the population would rapidly increase; which anticipations have happily come true. My whole capital, and more, was now sunk and disposed of. My mind at least in that respect was at rest; and it certainly looked as if the long-nursed scheme was about to be realized. In a few years the unearned increment was at least 100 per cent.; rents also went up surprisingly, and also, alas! the taxes. Unfortunately, within a year after completion of the building, and while I was in Caracas, Venezuela, an incendiary, a drunken gambler who had been running a "game" illicitly in one of the rooms, and who had been therefore turned out, deliberately used kerosene oil and set fire to the building. Result, a three-quarters' loss! Luckily I was well insured; even in the rentals, to the surprise of many people who had never heard of rental insurance before. The insurance settlement and payment was effected between myself and the agent in less than half an hour, and just as soon as I could get at it an architect was working on plans for a new structure. With the three months' loss on account of my absence, it was more than a year before the new building was ready for occupancy. It was, and is, a better-arranged and handsomer one than the old block, and its total rental is much greater.

BREAKING THE PRAIRIE.

FIRST CROP--MILO MAIZE.

The town has grown very much and seems to be permanently established. The building, and my affairs, are entirely in the hands of a responsible agent; and I am free to go where inclination calls. Nothing shall be said about the worries, the delays, the wage disputes, the lawsuits, etc., seemingly always in attendance on the erection of any building. Well, it is over now, and too sickening to think about! Nor shall much be said about the frequent calls on the property-owner to subscribe, to "put up," for any bonus the city may have decided to offer to secure the placing in "oor toon" of a State Methodist College, a State Hospital, a State Federal Building; or to induce a new railroad to build in; not to mention the securing for your own particular district of the town the site of a new court-house, a new post-office, etc. etc. The enmity caused by this latter contest is always bitter. But always anything to boost the town! This little town actually last year paid a large sum to the champion motor-car racer of America to give an exhibition in Amarillo. Even a flying-machine meeting was consummated, one of the first in the whole West.

In this plains country, such as surrounds Amarillo, during the land boom, immense tracts were bought by speculators, who then proceeded to dispose of it to farmers and small settlers. They do this on a methodical and grand scale. One such man chartered special trains to bring out from the middle States his proposed clients or victims. To meet the trains he owned as many as twenty-five motor-cars, in which at once on arrival these people were driven all over the property to make their selection.

The first breaking of this prairie country is done with huge steam ploughs, having each twelve shares, so that the breaking is done very rapidly, the depth cultivated being only some two inches or three inches. The thick close sod folds over most beautifully and exactly, and it was always a fascinating sight, if a sad one, to watch this operation--the first opening up of this soil that had lain uncultivated for so many aeons of time. The seed may be simply scattered on the sod before the breaking, and often a splendid crop is thus obtained. Simplicity of culture, truly!

Before leaving the United States of America a few notes about that country. Though as a rule physically unpicturesque, it has some great wonder-places and beauty spots, such as the Yosemite Valley, the Grand Canon of the Colorado, the Yellowstone Park, the Falls of Niagara, and the big trees of California, which trees it may be now remarked are conifers (Sequoia gigantea and Sequoia sempervirens), which attain a height of 400 feet. Sempervirens is so called because young trees develop from the roots of a destroyed parent.

If the reader has never seen these enormous trees he cannot well appreciate their immense altitude and dimensions. Remember that our own tallest and noblest trees in England do not attain more than 100 feet or so in height; then try to imagine those having four times that height and stems or trunks proportionately huge. It is like comparing our five-storey buildings with the forty-storey buildings of New York, eight times their altitude.

Yet these big trees are not so big as the gums of Australia; the Yellowstone Geysers are, or were, inferior to the like in New Zealand; and Niagara is surpassed by the Zambesi Falls, still more so by the waterfall in Paraguay, and infinitely so by the recently-discovered falls in British Guiana. The Guayra Falls, on the Parana River, in Paraguay, though not so high in one leap as Niagara, have twice as great a bulk of water, which rushes through a gorge only 200 feet wide.

Its cities, such as San Francisco, Chicago, St Louis, New Orleans and others, are not as a rule beautiful; even Washington, the capital, was a tremendous disappointment to my expectant gaze; though my judgment might possibly be affected by the following incident. While standing at the entrance of the extremely beautiful New Union Railway Station a cab drove up, out of which a woman stepped, followed by a man. He hurried after her, and right in front of me drew a pistol and shot her dead, and even again fired twice into her body as she lay on the ground. Then he quickly but coolly put the gun to his own head and killed himself.

This city seems badly planned and some of its great federal buildings are monstrous. The Pennsylvania Avenue is an eyesore and a disgrace to the nation. Boston, I believe, is all that it should be. Denver is a delightful town. New York, incomparable for its fabulous wealth, its unequalled shops, its magnificently and boldly-conceived office buildings and apartment blocks, its palatial and perfectly-appointed hotels, its dirty and ill-paved streets, is the marvel of the age and is every year becoming more so. Its growth continues phenomenal. If not now it will soon be the pulse of the world.

There is never occasion in American hotels, as there is in English, in my own experience, to order your table waiter to go and change his greasy, filthy coat or to clean his finger-nails! No, in the smallest country hotel in the United States the proprietor knows that his guests actually prefer a table servant to have clean hands, a clean coat, etc., and waiters in restaurants are obliged to wear thin, light and noiseless boots or shoes, not clodhoppers.

That phenomenon and much-criticized individual, the American child, is blessed with such bright intelligence that at the age of ten he or she is as companionable to the "grown-up" as the youth of twenty of other countries, and much more interesting.

English people are inclined to think Americans brusque and even not very polite. Let me assure them that they are the politest of people, though happily not effusive. They are also the most sympathetic and, strange as it may appear, the most sentimental. Their sympathy I have tested and experienced. Their brusqueness may arise from the fact that they have no time to give to formalities. But a civil question will always be civilly answered, and answered intelligently. Nor are Americans toadies or snobs; they are independent, self-reliant and self-respecting people.

CHAPTER X
FIRST TOUR ABROAD

Mexico--Guatemala--Salvador--Panama--Colombia--Venezuela--
Jamaica   --Cuba--Fire in Amarillo--Rebuilding.

Among the many long trips leisure has permitted, the first was a tour through Mexico, Guatemala and Salvador to Panama; thence through Colombia and Venezuela; Jamaica and Cuba; needless to say a most interesting tour. Mexico has a most delightful climate at any time of the year, except on the Gulf Coast, the Tierra Caliente, where the heat in summer is tropical and oppressive. She has many interesting and beautiful towns. The city itself is rapidly becoming a handsome one, indeed an imperial one. Accommodation for visitors, however, leaves much to be desired. The country's history is of course absorbingly interesting, and the many remains of Aztec and older origin appeal much to one's curiosity. There is a capital golf-course, a great bull-ring, and a pelota court. There is much wealth, and every evening a fine display of carriages and horses. The little dogs called Perros Chinos of Mexico, also "Pelon" or hairless, have absolutely no hair on the body. They are handsome, well-built little creatures, about the size of a small terrier. They are said to be identical with one of the Chinese edible dogs. Cortez found them in Mexico and Pizarro in Peru. How did they get there? Popocatepetl, a magnificent conical volcano, overlooks the city and plain. I tried to ascend it but a damaged ankle failed me. A trip to Oaxaca to see wonderful Mitla should not be missed. There also is the tree of Tuli, a cypress, said to measure 154 feet round its trunk. Also a trip to Orizaba city is equally interesting, if only for the view of the magnificent Pico de Orizaba, a gigantic and most beautiful cone 18,000 feet high; but also for the beautiful scenery displayed in the descent from the high plateau of Mexico, a very sudden descent of several thousand feet in fifteen miles, with a railroad grade of one in fourteen, from a temperate climate at once into a tropical one. More than that, it leads you to the justly-celebrated little Hotel de France in Orizaba, the only good hotel in all Mexico.

The imposing grandeur of a mountain peak depends of course greatly on its elevation above its base; for instance, Pike's peak, to the top of which I have been, is some 15,000 feet above sea-level, but only 8000 above its base. The great peaks of the Andes likewise suffer, such as Volcan Misti at Arequipa, nearly 20,000 feet above the sea, but from its base only 12,000 feet. Then imagine Orizaba peak at once soaring 16,000 feet above the city, not one of a chain or range, but proudly standing alone in her radiant beauty. From Orizaba I went on to Cordova, where it is the custom of the citizens of all ranks and ages to assemble in the evenings in the plaza to engage in the game of keeno or lotto. Many tables are laid out for the purpose. The prizes are small, but apparently enough to amuse the people. Of course I joined in the game, happened to be very successful, and as my winnings were turned over to some small boys, beautiful little black-eyed rascals, my seat was soon surrounded by a merry crowd and great was the fun. How beautiful and captivating are these Spanish and even Mestizo children, the boys even more so than their sisters. From this point I took train, over the worst-built and coggliest railroad track I ever travelled on, to the Isthmus of Tehuantepec, to see the famous Eads Route, over which he proposed to transport bodily, without breaking cargo, ocean-going sailing ships and steamers from the Gulf to the Pacific Ocean. Also to visit the Tehuana tribe of Indians, whose women have the reputation of being the finest-looking of native races in the Western world. They wear a most extraordinary and unique combined headdress and shawl. In the markets could certainly be seen wonderfully beautiful faces, quite beautiful enough to justify the claim mentioned. At Rincon is the starting-point of the projected and begun Pan-American railroad, which will eventually reach to Buenos Ayres. At Salina Cruz, the Pacific end of the isthmus, and I should think one of the windiest places on earth, perhaps beating even Amarillo, I met a young American millionaire, a charming man who had large interests in Guatemala. We sailed together from Salina Cruz on a small coasting steamer bound for Panama. Except only at Salina Cruz, where a terrific wind blows most of the year, the weather was calm, but the heat very great. Not even bed-sheets were provided, nor were they needed. Sailing by night we made some port and stopping-place every day. The view of the coast is most interesting. You are practically never out of sight of volcanoes, some of them of great height and many of them active. One particularly, Santa Maria, attracted our attention because of its erupting regularly at intervals of half an hour; regularly as your watch marked the stated period a great explosion occurred and a cloud of smoke, steam and dust was vomited out and floated away slowly landwards. In the clear calm air it was a magnificent spectacle and I never tired watching it. Another volcanic peak had recently been absolutely shattered, one whole side as it were blown off it. On arriving at San Jose, the port of Guatemala city, we had a great reception, my friend being the owner of the railroad--the only railroad in this State. A special train took us up to the capital, splendidly-horsed carriages were put at our disposal, and we were banqueted and entertained at the Opera, my friend insisting that I should share in all this hospitality. The American minister joined our party and made himself agreeable and useful. Guatemala city was once the Paris of America, was rich, gay and prosperous; to-day it is--different, but still very interesting. You are there in a bygone world, an age of the past. Revolutions and inter-State wars have driven capital from the country; progress is at a standstill; confidence in anybody does not exist. As in the Central American States, "Ote toi de la que m'y mette" is on the standard of every ambitious general, colonel or politician. It is the direct cause of all the revolutions. At Corinto a lady, whom we became intimate with, landed for the professed purpose of "revoluting." Yet the country is a naturally rich one, having on the highlands a splendid temperate climate, and everywhere great mineral and agricultural resources. We were fortunate to see a parade of some of the State troops; and such a comical picture of military imbecility and inefficiency could surely not be found elsewhere. The officers swaggered in the gayest of uniforms; the men were shoeless, dirty and slovenly. On approaching the city one passes near by the famous volcanoes Fuego, Aqua and Picaya (14,000 feet), and mysterious Lake Anatitlan.

A shooting-trip had been arranged for us: a steam launch on the lake, Indians as carriers, mules, etc. etc., but my friend declined for want of time. Among the fauna of the country are common and black jaguars, tapirs, manatees, peccaries, boas, cougars or pumas, and alligators. Also the quetzal, the imperial bird of the great Indian Quiche race, and the Trogan resplendens. Poinciana regia and P. pulcherrima are common garden shrubs or trees, but the finest Poinciana I ever saw was in Honolu-lu. Vampire bats are more common in Nicaragua, but also exist in Guatemala. They have very sharp incisors and bite cattle and horses on the back or withers, men on the toes if exposed, and roosters on the comb. They live in caves, and not as the large fruit bats of India, which repose head downwards, hanging from trees in great colonies. Vampires live on blood, having no teeth suitable for mastication.

It is a strange fact that Germans, who now have the great bulk of the trade throughout Central America, are very unpopular. Nor are the Americans popular. "Los Americanos son Bestias," "Esos Hombres son Demonios" express the feeling.

I was told that in Guatemala there exists a tribe of Indians which does not permit the use of alcoholic drink and actually pays the State compensation instead.

Among other places we called at were Esquintla, Acajutla, and La Libertad, from which point we got a magnificent view of the Atatlan volcano in full activity; also at San Juan del Sur. From Leon, in Nicaragua, some fourteen active volcanoes can be seen. In Salvador only two of the eleven great volcanoes of the State are now "*vivo*," viz., San Miguel and Izalco. The latter is called the Lighthouse of Salvador, because it explodes regularly every twenty minutes. The lesser living vents are called infernillos--little hells. Altogether it looks like Central America, as a whole, with its revolutions and its physical and political instability, must be a very big hell.

Salvador, though the smallest of the Central American States, is the most prosperous, enterprising and densely-populated. She was the first to become independent and the first to defy the Church of Rome.

It had been my intention to sail through Lake Nicaragua and down the river San Juan to San Juan del Norte. But accommodation at that port and steamer communication with Colon was so bad and irregular that the trip was regretfully abandoned, and I went on to Panama with my friend. This gentleman possessed a personal letter from President Roosevelt addressed to the canal officials, ordering (not begging) them to permit a full inspection of the works, and to tell the "truth and the whole truth." Consequently we saw the works under unusual and most favourable conditions. The Americans have made remarkable progress, assisted by their wonderful labour-saving appliances, chief among which are the 100-ton shovels, the Lidgerwood car-unloaders, and the track-shifters. But chiefly, of course, by their sanitary methods, the protection afforded the employees against mosquitoes, and the abolition of mosquito conditions. The natives and negroes are immune to yellow fever, but not to malaria. As most of us know, Major Ross of the I.M.S., in 1896, proved the connection of malaria with the anopheles mosquito; and in 1902 Mr Reed of the U.S. Health Commission tracked the yellow fever to the stegomyia mosquito. Yellow fever requires six days to develop. It should be noted that the stegomyia insect is common in India, but luckily has not yet been infected with the germ of yellow fever. And it may also be here mentioned that the connection between bubonic plague and rats, and the fleas that infest them, was discovered by the Japanese scientist, Kitasato.

The history of the canal may be touched on, if only to show the American method of securing a desired object, certainly a quick, effective and, after all, the only practical method. The Panama railway was built by Americans in 1855 to meet the rush to California gold-fields. The De Lesseps Company bought the road for an enormous figure, and started the canal works, to be abandoned later on, but again taken up by a new French Company. In 1901 Uncle Sam got his "fine work" in when he bluffed the new French Panama Company into selling it to him for 40,000,000 dollars, simply by threatening to adopt the Nicaragua route. Yet the Company's property was well worth the 100,000,000 dollars asked for it. To carry out the bluff, the Isthmian Canal Commission (U.S.) actually reported to Congress that the Nicaragua route was the most "practical and feasible" one, when it was well known to the Commission that the route was so impracticable as not to be worthy of consideration. At least common report had it so. In 1903 Colombia refused the United States offer to purchase the enlarged canal zone. At once Panama province seceded from the State, and sold the desired zone to the United States for 10,000,000 dollars, conditionally on the United States recognizing and guaranteeing the young Republic. The deal was cleverly arranged, and was again perhaps the only effective method to obtain possession.

The tide at Panama measures 20 feet, at Colon only 2 feet. In 1905 the International Board of Consulting Engineers, summoned by President Roosevelt, recommended, by eight to five, a sea-level canal (two locks). But Congress adopted the minority's 85-feet-level plan (6 locks), with an immense dam at Gatun, which dam will not be founded on rock, but have a central puddled core extending 40 feet below the bottom of the lake, and sheet piling some 40 feet still deeper. At least that is as I then understood it.

De Lesseps was not an engineer and knew little of science. His Company's failure was directly due to his ignorance and disregard of the advice of competent men.

Manual labour on the canal has been done mostly by Jamaica negroes. As said before, they are immune to yellow fever; and, speaking of the negro, it may be said here that his susceptibility to pain, compared to that of the white man, is as one to three, but the effect of a fair education is to increase it by one-third. What then is that of the monkey, the bird, the reptile or the fish? May I dare the statement, though most of us perhaps know it, that the sensitiveness of woman to that of man is as fifty-three to sixty-four. Even the woman's sense of touch, as in the finger-tips, being twice as obtuse as man's. The Bouquet D'Afrique, of course, is perceptible to us and offensive, but it is said that to the Indians of South America both black and white men are in this respect offensive. The "Foetor Judaiicus" must be noticeable also to have deserved the term.

But this is sad wandering from the subject in hand and not exactly "reminiscences." I only hope that this and other departures, necessary for stuffing purposes, may be excused, especially as they are probably the most entertaining part of the book.

To return to the town of Panama. In the bay and amongst the islands were quite a number of whales and flocks of pelicans. More curious to observe was an enormous number of small reddish-brown-coloured snakes, swimming freely on the surface of the sea, yet not seemingly heading in any particular direction. I could get no information regarding them. The famous Pearl Islands lie forty miles off Panama. The pearls are large and lustrous.

On reaching harbour the health officials came on board, and to my surprise selected me alone among the passengers for quarantine. The explanation was that I had gone ashore at Corinto. So I was ordered to take up my abode during the period of incubation in the detention house, a building in an isolated position; there I was instructed, much to my relief, that I might go to town or anywhere else during daylight, but must, under severe penalty, be back and inside the protecting screens before the mosquitoes got to work. The object was that no mosquito after biting me should be able to bite anyone else. We had been some two and a half days out of Corinto, so my period of detention was not of long duration. I also got infinitely better messing than any hotel in Panama afforded.

The seas on either side of Darien Isthmus were at one time the scene of the many brave but often cruel deeds of the great adventurers and explorers like Drake, buccaneers like Morgan, pirates like Kidd and Wallace. Morgan, a Welshman, sacked and destroyed old Panama, a rich and palatial city, in 1670. He also captured the strong fortress town, Porto Bello. Drake captured the rich and important Cartagena. Captain Kidd, native of Greenock, was commissioned by George III. to stamp out piracy, but turned pirate himself and became the greatest of them all.

It had been my intention to sail from Panama to Guayaquil, cross the Andes, and take canoe and steamer down the Amazon to Para. But the reports of yellow fever at Guayaquil, the unfinished state of the Quito railroad, and the disturbed state of the Trans-Andean Indians, through whose country there would be a week's mule ride, decided me to alter my plans once more. So, bidding good-bye to my very kind New York friend, who went home direct, I myself took steamer for a Colombian port and thence trained to Baranquillo, a considerable town on the Magdalena River. It was a novel experience to there find oneself a real live millionaire! The Colombian paper dollar (no coin used) was worth just the hundredth part of a gold dollar; so that a penny street car ride cost the alarming sum of five dollars, and dinner a perfectly fabulous amount. By Royal Mail steamer the next move was to La Guayra, the seaport of Caracas, a most romantic-looking place, where the mountains, some 9000 feet high, descend almost precipitously to the sea. There we saw the castle where Kingsley's Rose of Devon was imprisoned. At that time President Castro was so defying France that war and a French fleet were expected every day. Consequently his orders were that no one whomsoever should be allowed to enter the country. All the passengers of course, and for that very reason perhaps, were hoping to be allowed to land, if only to make the short run up to the capital and back. At Colon, assisted by my American friend and the United States consul, we "worked" the Venezuela Consul into giving me a passport (how it was done does not matter), which at La Guayra I, of course, produced. Of no avail! No one must land. But just when the steamer was about to sail a boat full of officials appeared at the steamer's side, called out my name, and lo! to the wonder of the other passengers, I was allowed to go ashore. This was satisfactory, and I at once took train to the capital, climbing or soaring as in a flying-machine the steep graded but excellent road (most picturesque) to Caracas. There I found that the Mardi Gras Carnival was just beginning. In my hotel was the war correspondent of the *New York Herald*, just convalescing from an attack of yellow fever and still incapable of active work. He was good enough to ask me to fill his place should hostilities ensue. No other correspondent was in the country and he himself had to put up a 10,000 dollar bond. I willingly agreed, and so stayed nearly two weeks in Caracas awaiting eventualities. During this time, owing to the Carnival, the town was "wide open"; every night some twenty thousand people danced in the Plaza Bolivar, a huge square beautifully paved with tiling. The dancers were so crowded together that waltzing simply meant revolving top-wise. A really splendid band provided the music. What a gay, merry people they are! And how beautiful these Venezuela women, and how handsome the men! In the streets presents of great value were tossed from the carriages to the signoras on the balconies. At a ball the men, the fashionables, wore blue velvet coats, not because of the season, but because it is the customary male festive attire. Caracas was delightful and extraordinarily interesting. What splendid saddle mules one here sees! Castro every day appeared with his staff all mounted on mules. All the traffic of the country is done with them, there being no feasible wagon roads. Castro had a most evil reputation. The people hated but feared him. His whole army consisted of Andean Indians, and he himself had Indian blood in his veins. The climate at Caracas is delightful. After two weeks and nothing developing, and not feeling quite well, I returned to La Guayra and took steamer back to Colon. Feeling worse on the steamer I called in the doctor, and was greatly alarmed when he pronounced yellow fever. On arriving at Colon, of course, I was not permitted to land so had to continue on the ship to Jamaica. The attack must have been a very mild one, as when we reached Jamaica I was nearly all right again.

Jamaica is a beautiful island with a delightful winter climate. Also very good roads. Among other places visited was Constant Spring Hotel, once the plantation residence and property of one of my uncles. At Port Antonio, on the north side of the island, is a very fine up-to-date American hotel, which of course was greatly appreciated after the vile caravanserais of Central America. Thence on to Cuba, the steamer passing through the famous narrows leading to Santiago. A pleasant daylight railroad run through the whole island brought me to the great city of Havana, not, as it appeared to me, a handsome or attractive city, but possessing a good climate and a polite and agreeable population. The principal shopping street in Havana is so narrow that awnings can be, and are, stretched completely across it. In the centre of the harbour was visible the wreck of the United States battleship *Maine*. Here in Havana, on calling at the Consulate for letters, or rather for cablegrams, as I had instructed my Amarillo agent not to write but to cable, and only in the case of urgent consequence, I found a message awaiting me. No need to open it therefore to know the contents! Yes, my building had been burnt to the ground two months ago. A cable to Caracas had not been delivered to me. So, back to Amarillo to view the ruins. In the United States of America one cannot insure for the full value of a building; or at least only three-quarters can be recovered. So my loss amounted to 8000 or 10,000 dollars. But no need of repining, and time is money, especially in such a case. So a new building was at once started, rushed and completed, in almost record time.

CHAPTER XI
SECOND TOUR ABROAD

Bermudas--Switzerland--Italy--Monte
Carlo--Algiers--Morocco--Spain--Biarritz and Pau.

In November 1907 I again left Amarillo bound for Panama and the Andes. But the only steamer offering from New Orleans was so small, and the messing arrangements so primitive, that I abandoned the idea, railed to New York, saw a steamer starting for the Bermudas and joined her. For honeymoon and other trips the Bermudas are a favourite resort of New Yorkers. Fourteen honeymoon couples were reckoned to be on board. The climate of these islands is very delightful. The hotels are quite good; English society pretty much confined to the Army and Navy; two golf-courses; the best of bathing, boating and sea-fishing. The Marine Aquarium is most interesting. The roads are good and not a motor-car in the land!

The islands are composed solely of coralline limestone. It can be quarried almost anywhere. Blasting is not necessary, the stone being so soft that it can be sawn out in blocks of any size to meet the architect's needs. It is beautifully white and hardens after exposure.

After staying two weeks I returned to New York and took passage to Cherbourg, crossed France to Lausanne, saw some friends and then went on to St Moritz, which we all know is so famous for its wonderful winter climate, intensely cold but clear skies and bright sunshine. Curling, hockey, skiing, tobogganing and bobbing were in full swing; the splendid hotels crowded; dinners and dances every day. A very jolly place indeed. After ten days' stay a sledge took me over the mountains to Chiavenna, thence steamer over the lake to Como, and train to Milan. It was very cold and foggy there, but the city is a handsome one; I saw the Cathedral, the arcade, etc., and visited the famous Scala Opera House and its wonderful ballet. Thence to Genoa--very cold--and on to Monte Carlo, at once entering a balmy, delicious climate. The season was just beginning, but the play-rooms were pretty full. With its splendid shops, fine hotels, gardens, Casino, pigeon-shooting, etc. etc., Monte Carlo is unrivalled. It is distinctly a place to wear "clothes," and the women's costumes in the play-rooms and Casino are enough to make the marrying man think twice.

After visiting Monaco, Nice and Cannes, at Marseilles I took steamer to Algiers. Barring its agreeable winter climate there is not much attraction there. Here I was told that the marriageable Jewess is kept in a dark room, fed on rich foods and allowed no exercise; treated, in fact, as a goose for a fat liver.

So I went on to Blida, where is a French Army Remount Depot. A large number of beautiful Arab horses were being inspected and shown by their picturesque owners. They were not the type for cow-ponies and seemed a bit light for cavalry purposes. From Blida I went by train to Oran, a considerable port in Algiers. There was nothing particular to see or do except visit a certain Morocco chief who had started the late troubles at Fez and was here in durance vile (chains). Among the few tourists I met a Hungarian and his English wife and we became fairly intimate. His wife told me he was the dread of her life, being scorching mad on motor-cars. It happened there was one and only one car in the town for hire, and the Baron must needs hire it and invite me, with his wife, to a trip up a certain hill or mountain overlooking the city. A holy man, or marabout, denned on the top and we must pay our respects. The road proved to be exceedingly steep, and zigzagged in a remarkable way, with very sharp, angular turns. No car had ever been up it, and few carriages. We reached the top in due time, saluted the old man and started back. My friend was at the wheel and did a few turns all right, till we came to a straight shoot, very narrow, a ditch on one side, trees on the other, and just here the brake refused to work. Reaching over I touched his shoulder and suggested that he should go slower. No reply; he was speechless, and we knew at once that he had lost control, and realized our horrible position. On we rushed, he guiding it straight all right, till we approached the bend, the worst on the road, and quite impossible to manipulate at great speed. Right in front was an unguarded cliff, with a drop of 500 feet over practically a precipice. But--well, there was no "terrible accident" to be reported. Most fortunately a pile of rocks had been accumulated for the purpose of building a parapet wall, and on to the top of this pile the car jumped and lodged, without even turning over. The jar and shock were bad enough, but no one was much hurt. It reminded me of another occasion when I got a jar of a different kind. Once, after playing golf with a man in America, he offered to drive me to town in his motor-car. Knowing him to be a scorcher I excused myself by saying that I was not ready to go. He started; very soon afterwards word came back that he had run into a telegraph post and killed himself and his driver. Such things tend to cool one's motor ambition.

At Oran I boarded a small French steamer for Mellilla, in Spanish Morocco, a Spanish convict station and a considerable military post. This was just before Spain's recent Riff Campaign. The table fare on the steamer was not British! Cuttle-fish soup or stew was prominent on the bill; a huge dish of snails was always much in demand, and the other delicacies were not tempting, to me at least. Eggs, always eggs! How often in one's travels does one have to resort to them. In Mellilla itself there was no hotel. We messed at the strangest restaurant it was ever my ill-luck to enter. The troops reminded me somewhat of those of Guatemala, slovenly, slouching, and poorly dressed. Their officers were splendid in gold braid, feathers and gaudy uniforms. Around the town were circular block-houses, beyond which even then no one was allowed to go. Indeed, mounted tribesmen could be seen sometimes riding up to the line and flourishing their guns in apparent defiance. Curiosity made me venture forward till warned back by the guard. These Riffians were certainly picturesque-looking rascals. Mellilla was then not on the tourist's track, so was all the more interesting and novel.

From there by steamer to Gibraltar, stopping at Ceuta on the way. At Gibraltar a friend, Capt. B----, took me all over the rock, the galleries, and certain fortifications. A meeting of hounds near Algeciras was attended. Thence by train to Granada to visit the marvellously lovely Alhambra, and of course to meet the King of the Gipsies; Ronda, romantic and picturesque; Cordova and its immense mosque and old Roman bridge; and so on to Madrid by a most comfortable and fast train; but the temperature all through Central Spain is extremely cold in winter. The country is inhospitable-looking, and the natives seem to have abandoned their picturesque national dress. One must now go to Mexico to see the cavalier in his gay and handsome costume. In Madrid I of course visited the splendid Armoury; also the National Art Gallery with its Velasquezs and Murillos. From Madrid to San Sebastian, the season not yet begun, and Biarritz. Here I spent a most enjoyable month: dry, bracing climate, good golf-course, good hotels, etc. It was the English season; the Spanish season being in summer. On King Edward's arrival with his entourage and fashionable followers golf became impossible, so I went on to Pau and played there. From Pau a short run took me to Lourdes, with its grotto, chapel, etc. From Pau to Bordeaux, a handsome, busy town. Then Paris and home.

CHAPTER XII
THIRD TOUR ABROAD

Salt Lake City--Canada--Vancouver--Hawaii--Fiji--Australia--New Zealand--Tasmania--Summer at Home.

The fall of 1908 saw me off on a tour which finally took me round the world. Space will only permit of its itinerary and a few of my impressions and experiences. From Amarillo I trained north to Salt Lake City, passing through the wonderful gorge of the Arkansas River and the canon of the Grand; scenery extremely wild and impressive. At Salt Lake found a large, busy, up-to-date city. Visited the tabernacle, and heard the great organ, the largest in the world; and a very fine choir. The acoustics of this immense and peculiarly-shaped building are most perfect. The Temple Gentiles are not allowed to enter. Outside the irrigation limits the country has a most desolate, desert, hopeless aspect. What nerve the Mormons had to penetrate to such a spot.

It may be noted here that one Sidney Rigdon was the compiling genius of Mormonism; and it was he who concocted the Mormon Bible, not Joe Smith. And what a concoction! No greater fraud was ever perpetrated.

Hence by Butte, Montana, the great copper-mining city, to Great Falls, where we crossed the Missouri River, there 4000 miles from the sea, yet twice as large as the Thames at Windsor. On entering Canadian territory a remarkable change in the character of the people, the towns and the Press was at once noticeable. From Calgary by the C.P.R. the trip through the Selkirk range to Vancouver was one of continuous wonder and delight--noble peaks, dense pine forests, rushing rivers and peaceful lakes. Arrived at Vancouver city, a city of illimitable ambition and bright prospects. I there met in the lobby of the hotel two very old friends whom I had not seen for many years. They dined with me, or rather wined and dined, and we afterwards spent a probably uproarious evening. I say probably, because the end was never evident to me till I woke up in my bed, whither someone had carried me, with my stockinged foot burning in a candle; another such illuminant had been lighted and placed at my head. My waking (and I was "waked" in two senses) endangered, and at the same time prevented, the probable burning down of the building. Next morning I was taken suddenly ill, but not due to the evening's carousal, so went across the bay to Victoria and hunted up a doctor, who immediately ordered me into hospital (the Victoria Jubilee) and operated on me the very same day. The operation was the most painful that I have ever undergone but was entirely successful, though it detained me in the hospital for over a month.

From Victoria I trained to San Francisco, passing through lovely Washington and Oregon States, and Northern California; and from San Francisco took steamer to Honolulu. San Francisco was rising from its ashes, but still presented a terrible aspect, and gave a good idea of how appalling the catastrophe must have been. At Honolulu I spent a most enjoyable two weeks, golfing a little, surf riding, etc. The climate is ideal, hotels are good, parts of the islands lovely. They are all volcanic, and indeed some are nothing but an agglomeration of defunct craters.

On one of the islands, Maui, is the largest crater on earth (unless perhaps a certain one in Japan), its dimensions being 2000 feet in depth, eight miles wide, and situated on the top of a mountain, Haleakala, 10,000 feet high. Its surface, seen from the rock-rim, exactly resembles that of the moon. I of course also visited the largest island of the group--Hawaii--passing *en route* Molokai, the leper settlement. Hawaii has two very high volcanic mountains, Mauna Kea and Mauna Loa, some 13,000 feet. The land is very prolific, the soil consisting of pulverized lava and volcanic dust, whose extreme fertility is due to a triple proportion of phosphates and nitrogen. On the slope of Mauna Loa is the crater of Kilauea, and in its centre the "pit," called Haleamaumau, the most awe-inspiring and in other ways the most remarkable volcano in the world. Landing at Hilo, by train and stage we went to see it. My visit was made at night when the illumination is greatest. Traversing the huge crater, four miles in diameter, the surface devoid of all vegetation, seamed and cracked, and in places steam issuing from great fissures, we suddenly arrived at the brink of the famous pit, and what an astonishing sight met our gaze! The sheer walls of the circular pit were some 200 feet deep: the diameter of the pit one quarter of a mile: the contents a mass of (not boiling, for what could the temperature be!) restless, seething, molten, red-hot lava, rising from the centre and spreading to the sides, where its waves broke against the walls like ocean billows, being a most brilliant red in colour! Flames and yet not flames. Now and then geysers of fire would burst through the surface, shoot into the air and fall back again. The sight was to some people too awful for prolonged contemplation, myself feeling relieved as from a threat when returning to the hotel, but still with a desire to go back and again gaze into that awful maelstrom. The surface of the pit is not stationary, at one time being, as then, sunk 200 feet; another time flush with the brim and threatening destruction; and again almost disappearing out of sight. At any time and in whatever condition it is an appalling spectacle and one never to be forgotten.

Sugar and pineapples are the main products of the islands; but one should not miss visiting the aquarium at Honolulu to see the collection of beautiful and even comical-looking native fishes; some of extravagant colouring, brilliant as hummingbirds, gay as butterflies; of shapes unsuspected, and in some cases indescribable, having neither length nor breadth, depth nor thickness; hard to distinguish head from tail, upside from underside; speed being apparently the least desirable of characteristics. Do they depend for protection and safety on their grotesque appearance? or do their gaudy robes disarm and enchant their ferocious and cannibalistic brethren?

One of the funniest sights I ever saw was a base-ball game played here between Chinese and Japanese youngsters. What a commanding position these islands occupy in ocean navigation, as a coaling or naval station, or as a distributing point. America was quick to realize this; and now splendid harbours and docks are being constructed, and the place strongly fortified so as to rival Gibraltar.

In January 1909 I joined the new and delightful New Zealand Steamship Company's steamer *Makura* bound for Sydney. On board was, amongst a very agreeable company, a gentleman bound for New Zealand on a fishing-trip, who told me such marvellous tales of his fishing prowess in Scotland that I put him down for one of the biggest liars on earth. More of him afterwards. Also on board was a young English peer, Earl S----, a very agreeable man, whose company I continued to enjoy for the greater part of this tour. We had a delightful passage, marred for me, however, by a severe attack of neuritis, which continued for three solid months, the best doctors in Sydney and Melbourne failing to give relief. Our ship first called at Fanning Island, a cable station (delivering four months' mail), a mere coral atoll with its central lagoon, fringe of cocoanut trees and reef. The heavy swell breaking on the reef, and the wonderful blue of the water, the peaceful lagoon, the bright, clear sky, and the cocoanut trees, formed a picture never to be forgotten. A picture typical of all the many thousands of such Pacific islets. After passing the Union and Wallace groups we crossed the 180 deg. meridian, and so lost a day, Sunday being no Sunday but Monday. Then arrived at Suva, Fiji Islands. The rainy season having just begun it was very hot and disagreeable. The Fijians are Papuans, but tall and not bad-looking. Maoris, Hawaiians and Samoans are Polynesians, a much handsomer race. The Fijians were remarkable for their quick conversion to devout Christianity. So late as 1870 cannibalism was general. Prisoners were deliberately fattened to kill. The dead were even dug up when in such a condition that only puddings could be made of them. Limbs were cut off living victims and cooked in their presence; and even more horrible acts were committed. The islands are volcanic, mountainous, and covered by forests.

Our visit was about the time of the Balolo worm season. The Balolo worm appears on the coast punctually twice a year, once in October (the Little Balolo) and once about the 20th November (the Great Balolo). They rise to the sea surface in writhing masses, only stay twelve hours and are gone. The natives make a great feast of them. The worm measures 2 ins. to 2 ft. long, is thin as vermicelli and has many legs. Never is a single worm seen at any other time.

Leaving Fiji, we passed the Isle of Pines, called at Brisbane, and arrived at Sydney on the 25th November. Of the beauties and advantages of Sydney Harbour we have all heard, and I can only endorse the glowing descriptions of other writers. Hotels in Australia and New Zealand are very poor, barring perhaps one in Sydney and a small one in Melbourne. A great cricket match was "on"--Victoria versus New South Wales--so I must needs go to see, not so much the game itself as the very famous club ground, said to be the finest in the world. In the Botanical Gardens, near a certain tree, the familiar, and I thought the unmistakable, odour of a skunk was most perceptible. Hailing a gardener and drawing his attention to it, he replied that the smell came from the tree ("malotus" he called it), but the crushed leaves, the bark and the blossom certainly gave no sign of it and I remained mystified. Fruit of many kinds is cheap, abundant and good. Sydney is not a prohibition town! Far from it. Drink conditions are as bad as in Scotland. Many of the people, especially from the country, have a pure Cockney accent and drop their h's freely; indeed I met boys and girls born in the colony, and never out of it, whose Cockney pronunciation was quite comical. It struck me that Australians and New Zealanders are certainly not noted for strenuousness.

Of course the tourist must see the Blue Mountains, and my trip there was enjoyable enough, I being greatly impressed with the Leura and other waterfalls (not as falls) and the wonderful and beautiful caves of Janolan. Wild wallabies were plentiful round about, and the "laughing jackass" first made himself known to me.

February 2nd.--S---- and myself took passage to New Zealand, the fish-story man being again a fellow-traveller. During the crossing numerous albatrosses were seen. In New Zealand we visited all the great towns, Wellington, Auckland, Christchurch, Dunedin and others, all of them pleasant, agreeable places, Christchurch being especially attractive. What a grand, healthy, well-fed and physically fit-looking people the New Zealanders are. Scotch blood predominates, and really there is a great similarity between the two peoples. At Rotorua we met the Premier and other celebrities, S---- being very interested in Colonial politics. Rotorua is a very charming place; I did some fishing in the lake, where trout were so numerous that it was not much sport catching them. Illness unfortunately prevented my going further afield and fishing for larger trout in the rivers. A Colonel M---- and sister who were in New Zealand at that time claimed to have beaten the record, their catch averaging over 20 lbs. per fish (rainbows), as they told me on again meeting them in the Hebrides. We did the Wanganui River of course; and the geysers at Whakarewarewa, under the charge of Maggie, the Maori guide.

As you no doubt are aware, the Maori fashion of salutation is to rub noses together. As long as they are pretty noses there cannot be much objection; but some of the Maori girls are themselves so pretty that mere rubbing is apt to degenerate and one's nose is liable to slip out of place. Maggie, the Maori guide, a very pretty woman and now at Shepherd's Bush, can tell all about it and even give a demonstration.

Here in Whakarewarewa one is impressed with the fact that this little settlement is built on what is a mere shallow crust, under which, at the depth of only a few feet, is a vast region of boiling mud and water. Everywhere around are bubbling and spluttering mud-wells, some in the form of miniature geysers; steam is issuing everywhere from clefts and crannies in the ground; and one almost expects a general upheaval or sinking of the whole surface. The principal geyser was not and had not been for some weeks in action. It can be forced into action, however, by the singular method of dropping a bar of soap down the orifice, when a tremendous rush of steam and water is vomited out with terrific force. Sir Joseph Ward, the Premier, is the only person authorized to permit this operation: but though he was at our hotel, and we were personally intimate with him, he declined to favour us with the permission, it being explained that the too-frequent dosing of the geyser had seemed to have a relaxing effect on the activity.

At Dunedin S---- left me to visit Milford Sound. Too unwell to accompany him, I continued on to the Bluff and then took steamer to Hobart, Tasmania. New Zealand has a great whale-fishery and it was my hope to see something of it by a short trip on one of the ships employed; but the opportunity did not present itself.

May I here offer a few notes picked up on the subject of whales, etc. The sperm or cachalot whale is a dangerous and bold fighter and is perhaps the most interesting of all cetaceans. His skin, like that of the porpoise, is as thin as gold-beaters' leaf. Underneath it is a coating of fine hair or fur, not attached to the skin, and then the blubber. He has enormous teeth or tushes in the lower jaw, but has no baleen. He devours very large fish, even sharks, but his principal food seems to be cuttle-fish and squids, some of them of as great bulk as himself. These cuttle-fish's tentacle discs are as big as soup-plates, and surrounded by hooks as large and sharp as tiger claws; while their mouths are armed with a parrot-like beak capable of rending anything held to them by the tentacles. These disc hooks are often found in ambergris, an excretion of the sperm whale. The sperm whale spouts diagonally, other whales upwards. So-called porpoise leather is made of the skin of the white whale. The porpoise is the true dolphin, the sailor's dolphin being a fish with vertical tail, scales and gills. Bonitoes are a species of mackerel, but warm-blooded and having beef-like flesh.

Near Hobart I saw the famous fruit and hop lands on the Derwent River. It was midsummer here and extremely hot, hotter than in Melbourne or anywhere else on this trip. From Hobart I railed to Launceston and thence steamer to Melbourne.

Melbourne is a very handsome city as we all know. It was my hope to continue on with S---- north by the Barrier Reef, or rather between the reef and the mainland, and so on to China, Japan, Corea, and home by Siberia; but my doctor advised me not to attempt it, so I booked passage for Colombo instead, and S---- and myself necessarily parted. But it was with much regret that I missed this wonderful coasting trip, long looked forward to and now probably never to be accomplished. On my way home I visited beautiful Adelaide, and the younger city, Perth, which reminded me much of the West American mining towns. Colombo needs no call for notice. At Messina we saw the ruined city, the devastation seeming to have been very terrible; but it presented no such awful spectacle of absolutely overwhelming destruction as did San Francisco. Etna was smoking; Stromboli also. Then Marseilles, Paris, and home.

During that summer at home I was fortunate enough to see the polo test matches between Hurlingham and Meadowbrook teams, otherwise England versus America. It was a disheartening spectacle. The English could neither drive a ball with accuracy nor distance; they "dwelt" at the most critical time, were slow in getting off, overran the ball, and in fact were beaten with ease, as they deserved to be.

An even more interesting experience was a visit to the aviation meeting at Rheims, the first ever held in the world, and a most successful one. Yet the British Empire was hardly represented even by visitors. Such great filers as Curtis, Lefevre, Latham, Paulhan, Bleriot and Farman were all present.

In the autumn I had a week's salmon-fishing at Garynahine in the Lews. The weather was not favourable and the sport poor considering the place. Close by is the Grimersta river and lodge, perhaps the finest rod salmon fishery in Scotland. A young East Indian whom I happened to know had a rod there, and was then at the lodge. On asking him about fishing, etc., he told me, and showed me by the lodge books, that the record for this river was fifty-four salmon in one day to one rod, all caught by the fly! The fortunate fisherman's name? Mr Naylor! the very man I had travelled with to New Zealand! I have vainly tried for three seasons now to get a rod on this river, if only for a week, and at L30 a week that would be long enough for me. I also this autumn had a rod on the Dee, but only fished twice; no fish and no water. During this summer I golfed very determinedly, buoyed up by the vain hope of becoming a first-class player--a "scratch" man. Alas! alas! but it is all vanity anyway! What does the angler care for catching a large basket of trout if there be no one by to show them to? And what does the golfer care about his game if he have not an opponent or a crowd to witness his prowess? At Muirfield I enjoyed the amateur championship--R. Maxwell's year.

CHAPTER XIII
FOURTH TOUR ABROAD

Yucatan--Honduras--Costa
Rica--Panama--Equador--Peru--Chile--Argentina--Brazil--
Teneriffe.

Octtober 1909 saw me on board the steamer *Lusitania*, bound for New York and another long trip somewhere. What a leviathan! What luxury! Think of the Spanish dons who crossed the same ocean in mere cobble boats of fifty tons, and our equally intrepid discoverers and explorers. What methods did they adopt to counteract the discomfort of *mal de mer*? Which reminds me that on this same *Lusitania* was the Viscomte D----, Portuguese Ambassador or Minister to the United States of America, who confidentially told me that he at one time was the worst of sailors, but since adopting a certain belt which supports the diaphragm the idea of sea-sickness never even suggests itself to him. For the public benefit it may be said that this belt is manufactured by the Anti Mal de Mer Belt Co., National Drug and Chemical Co., St Gabriel Street, Montreal, Canada. Bad sailors take note! On this steamer were also, as honoured guests, Jim Jeffries, the redoubtable, going to his doom; "Tay Pay" O'Connor; and Kessler, the "freak" Savoy Hotel dinner-giver; also, by the way, a certain London Jew financier, who gave me a commission to go to and report on the Quito railroad.

When travelling west from New York in the fall one is filled with admiration for the wonderful colour of the maple and other trees. Europe has nothing at all comparable. This wonderful display is alone worth crossing the Atlantic to see.

I found that the past summer had been a record hot one for Texas. The thermometer went to 115 deg. in the shade. Eggs were cooked (fried, it is to be supposed) on the side-walk, and popcorn popped in the stalks. In November I sailed from New Orleans for Yucatan to visit at Merida a Mexican friend, who turned out to be the King of Yucatan, as he was popularly called, he being an immense landed proprietor and practically monopolist of the henequin industry. Henequin, or Sisal hemp, is the fibre of *Agave Sisalensis*, a plant very like the *Agave Americana*, from which pulque is extracted. Thence round the corner, so to speak, to British Honduras, where we called in at Belize, whose trade is in mahogany and chicklee gum, combined with a deal of quiet smuggling done with the Central American States. Quite near Belize, among the innumerable islands and reefs, was the stronghold of the celebrated pirate Wallace (Scotchman). Many man-o'-war birds and pelicans were in the harbour. From Belize to Porto Barrios, the eastern terminus of the Guatemala railway. Here we are close to the scene of that wonderful and mysterious Central American prehistoric civilization, which has left for our antiquarians and learned men a life-work to decipher the still dumb symbols carved on its stupendous ruins. In Guatemala, and near this railway, are Copan and Quirigua, and probably other still undiscovered dead cities. Some of these Guatemala structures show a quite extraordinary resemblance to those at Angkor in Cambodia. Mitla and Palenque are in Mexico and are equally remarkable. The latter is still difficult to get to. Here again (Palenque) the temple shows a strange similarity to that at Boro Budoer in Java. Was it Stamford Raffles who said that, as far as the expenditure of human labour and skill goes, the pyramids of Egypt sink into insignificance when compared with this sculptured temple of Boro Budoer. Chichen-Itza, Labna, Sayil and Uxmal are all in Yucatan and approached from Merida. How many more of such very wonderful ruins are still hidden in the dense jungle of these countries it will be many years yet before we may know. Some I have seen myself, and it is still my hope very soon to visit others.

Among the wild animals of Yucatan and Honduras are the jaguar (*Felis onca*) with spots, ocellated or eyed; and the panther (*Felis concolor*) called puma in Arizona; the vaca de aqua or manatee, shaped like a small whale but with two paddles; the howling monkey, largest in America, and the spider monkey; the iguana, largest land lizard known to history, and alligators. Alligators are confined to the Western Hemisphere; crocodiles were supposed to be peculiar to the East, but lately a true crocodile (*Crocodilus Americanus*) has been identified in Florida. The alligator covers its eggs with a heap of rubbish for warmth and so leaves them; the African crocodile, on the contrary, buries them in the sand and then sits over them. The cardinal bird and the ocellated turkey must not be forgotten. Here may be found the leaf-cutting ants, which store the leaf particles in order to grow a fungus on, and which they are very particular shall be neither too damp nor too dry. Also another ant, the *Polyergus Rufescens*, a pure slave-hunter, absolutely dependent on its slaves for all the comforts of life and being even fed by them.

In Honduras there are many Caribs, still a strong race of Indians, having a strict and severe criminal law of their own. They are employed mostly as mahogany cutters, and are energetic, intelligent and thoroughly reliable workmen. Puerto Cortez in Honduras has the finest harbour on the whole Atlantic coast of Central America.

Note.--St Thomas is supposed to have visited and civilized the Central American Indians, as Quetzalcohuatl did in Mexico.

On leaving New Orleans it had been my intention to enter Nicaragua and report to a certain New Orleans newspaper on the conditions in that most distressful country; said paper having commissioned me to do so. Entrance to the State could only be made from Guatemala, but that country's consul in New Orleans refused to issue the necessary passport. Had I gone as an Englishman, and not as an American, there might have been no difficulty. As said before, Central American States have a dread and suspicion of Yankees. This was at the time that two Yankee revolutionists had been shot by the President of Nicaragua.

The next place of call was Limon, the port of Costa Rica. Every foot of land on these coasts, suitable for the growth of bananas, has been bought up by the great American Fruit Co., a company of enormous resources and great enterprise. Limon is a delightful little town from whence the railway runs to San Jose, the capital, which stands some 4000 feet above sea-level. Costa Rica is a peace-loving little state, prosperous, and enjoying a delightful climate. Much coffee and cocoa is grown, shaded by the Bois immortel or madre de Cacao. The live-stock industry is also a large one, and the animals seen on the high grassy plains are well grown and apparently well bred enough. I visited Cartago, a city which soon afterwards was destroyed by an earthquake.

On the railroad trip up to and back from the capital we passed through lovely and romantic scenery, high hills, deep ravines and virgin tropical forest. The rainy season was at its height, and how it rained! The river was a raging torrent, and from the railway "cut" alongside continuous land-slides of loose gravelly soil were threatening the track with demolition. Indeed, at some points this had actually occurred, and the train several times had to be stopped to allow the gangs of workmen to clear the way. A bad slide, had it hit the train, would have pushed the whole thing into the deep and turbulent river. All the passengers were much alarmed, and I stood on the car platform ready to jump, though the jump would necessarily have been into the seething water.

November 27th.--Colon once more! Went on to Panama. The Chagres River was in the highest state of flood known in twenty years.

November 30th.--Sailed on steamship *Chile* with about thirty passengers, all Spanish Americans, bound for Equador, Peru or Chile.

December 3rd.--Reached the Equator, and I donned warmer clothes. We saw whales, sharks, porpoises, rays and thrashers. Entered the Guayaquil River. Here was where Pizarro first landed and obtained a footing. The steamer anchored in quarantine a mile below the city. Yellow fever was raging as usual, and the Quito railroad was blocked by the revolutionists, so my projected visit again for the second time fell through. Guayaquil has the highest permanent death-rate of all cities. The state produces much cocoa and mangrove wood. The town is the centre of the Panama hat trade, which hats are made of the sheaths of the unexpanded leaves of the jaraca palm, or of the long sheaths protecting the flower-cone of the hat palm (*taquilla*); and they can only be made in a favourable damp atmosphere. Here on the mangrove roots and submerged branches enormous quantities of oysters may be found. Oysters on trees at last! Belonging to Equador State are the Galapagos Islands, 500 miles westward. Of course we did not visit them, but they are remarkable for their giant tortoises and their wild cattle, donkeys and dogs. It is said that these dogs do not bark, having forgotten how to; but they develop the power after contact with domestic ones. The Guayaquil River swarms with alligators, but luckily the alligator never attacks man.

We sailed south down the coast, calling at many ports. From Guayaquil south to Valparaiso, a distance of 2000 miles, we enjoyed bright, clear weather, a pleasant, sometimes an even too low temperature, and peaceful seas, a condition which the captain assured me was constant, the low temperature being due to the South Polar or Humboldt current. The absolute barren condition of this whole coast is also indirectly due to this current, the temperature of the sea being so much below that of the land that evaporation and condensation do not take place. After passing some guano islands on December 9th we landed at Callao, the port of Lima. Went on to Lima, a city founded by Pizarro, and once a very gay, luxurious and licentious capital. It is celebrated for its handsome churches. Its streets are narrow and the whole population seemingly devoted to peddling lottery tickets. There are many Chinamen amongst its 150,000 inhabitants. The Roman Catholics control the country, which is absolutely priest-ridden, Reformed or other churches not being permitted in Peru. A revolution was attempted only a few days ago, the President having been seized and dragged out of his office to be shot. The military, however, rescued him and the revolution was over in twenty-four hours. Peru's resources, outside of the very rich mining districts, will eventually be found in the Montana country, on the lower eastern slopes of the Andes. Her people are backward, and, at least in Cuzco and Arequipa, I should say the dirtiest in the world. There is as yet little or no tourist traffic on this coast; and there will not be much till better steamers are put on and hotels improved. In Lima, however, the Hotel Maury is quite good, though purely Spanish. It never rains on this coast, yet Lima is foggy and cold.

I took a trip up to Oroya over the wonderful Meiggs railway. M. Meiggs was an American, who had to leave his country on account of certain irregularities. We reached a height of 16,000 feet, the country being absolutely barren and devoid of vegetation, but very grand and imposing.

December 16th.--Sailed from Callao for Mollendo, calling at Pisco. Here, close to the harbour, are wonderful guano islands, on two of which were dense solid masses of birds covering what seemed to be hundreds of acres of ground. How many millions or billions must there have been! And yet, it being the evening, millions more were flighting home to the islands. With glasses they could be seen in continuous files coming from all directions. These birds are principally cormorants and pelicans. There are also very many seals, and we saw some whales. These islands presented one of the most marvellous sights I ever saw. And what enormous, still undeveloped, fisheries there must be here to support this bird-life. To-day we also passed a field of "Red Sea," confervae or infusoria. We were favoured for once

LLAMAS AS PACK ANIMALS.

with a grand view of the Andean peaks, which are seldom well seen from the coast, being wrapped in haze and clouds.

Arrived at Mollendo, port of Arequipa and Bolivia, I at once took train and rose rapidly to an elevation of 8000 feet, arriving in the evening at Arequipa. The whole country is desolate in the extreme. On the high plains we passed through an immense field of moving sand-hills, all of crescent shape, the sand being white and of a very fine grain. On approaching Arequipa the sunset effect on the bright and vari-hued rock strata and scoriae, backed by the grand Volcan Misti, 19,000 feet high, made a marvellously beautiful picture, the most beautiful of its kind ever seen by me, and showing how wonderfully coloured landscapes may be without the presence of vegetation of any kind. Hotels in Arequipa are very primitive, and after a glance at the market and its filthy people you will confine your table fare to eggs and English biscuits as I did. Arequipa has been thrice destroyed by earthquakes and is indeed considered the quakiest spot on earth. Priests, monks, ragged soldiers and churches almost compose the town; yet it has a very beautiful Plaza de Armas, where in the evenings Arequipa fashion promenades to the music of a quite good band. I seemed to be the only tourist here.

On the 20th I took train to Juliaca, rising to 15,000 feet; thence two days to Cuzco, the celebrated southern capital of the Incas, whose history I will not here touch on. Not only are there abandoned Inca remains, but also in high Peru and Bolivia remains of structures erected, as it is now supposed, 5000 years ago. The pottery recently found would suggest this, it being as gracefully moulded and decorated as that of Egypt of the same period; authority even declaring it to be undistinguishable from the latter, and they also testify to evidence of an extremely high and cultivated civilization, not barbaric in any sense, in these remote periods. Indeed, the civilization of the country at that far-off time must have been quite as advanced as in the Nile Valley. Cyclopean walls and other remains show a marvellous skill in construction; individual blocks of granite-stone, measuring as much as fifteen to twenty feet in diameter, being placed in these walls with such skill that even to-day a pen-knife blade cannot be inserted between them. No mortar was used, but the blocks are keyed together in a peculiar way. How this stone was so skilfully cut and transported we cannot imagine; even with iron and all our modern appliances it is doubtful if we could produce such exactitude.

DRIFTING SAND DUNE. (One of thousands.)

At Puna one gets a good view of Lake Titicaca, still a large lake, but once of much greater dimensions. Sailing over and among the high peaks it was here my good fortune to view for the first time that majestic bird, the condor, which, it is declared, has never been seen to flap its wings. Thus in the South Seas I had been privileged to see the albatross, and here the condor. Lucky, indeed, to have viewed these monarchs of the air, free in their proper element, in all their pride, grace and beauty. How often, as a boy, or even as a man, has one anticipated "some day" seeing these noble birds in their native haunts! Also many llamas and alpacas, the former very handsome animals. The vicunas and guanacos are the wild representatives of this family, and are also very abundant. In Arequipa I suffered somewhat from "nevada," due to electric conditions, and distinct from "saroche." Saroche never affected me.

December 27th.--Sailed for Valparaiso, calling at Iquique, Antofagasta and Coquimbo. The coast country is so desolate and arid that at some of these purely nitrate towns school-children's knowledge of trees and other plants is derived solely from painted representations on boardings erected for the purpose. This may seem libellous, but is not so.

We arrived at Valparaiso on New Year's Day. The city showed few signs of its late disaster. The harbour is poor, and the place has few attractions. Society was attending a race meeting at Vino del Mar. Went on to Santiago, the capital, 1500 feet elevation, population claimed 300,000; our route lying through rich, well-cultivated valleys. The climate and general appearance of the country are much like those of California, the temperature being quite hot at mid-day but cool always in the shade, the nights being chilly. This was midsummer. Santiago has some handsome buildings and a very attractive Plaza Mayor; the hotels are poor. The Chilians are an active, intelligent, wide-awake people; are great fighters and free from the religious trammels of Peru. From here I took train to Los Andes; then by narrow gauge line, the grade being 7 per cent. on the cog track, through barren rough gorges to the Cumbre, or summit, 13,000 feet high. The most commanding peak that we saw was Aconcagua, over 23,000 feet high, and the highest mountain in the Western Hemisphere. At Lago del Inca, at the entrance to the incompleted tunnel, we left the train and took mules or carts to the summit, where is an immense, surprising and commanding figure of the Christ. On the Argentina side we again took train to

PERUVIAN RUINS. (Note dimensions of stones and locking system)

Mendoza, an important town and centre of the fruit and wine country. Thence a straight run over the immense level pampas, now pastures grazed by innumerable cattle, sheep and horses, to Buenos Ayres. Many rheas (ostriches) were seen from the train. These birds, the hens, lay in each other's nests, and the male incubates-- perhaps to save the time of the hens; which reminds one of the cuckoo, who mates often, and whose stay is so limited that she has no time to incubate. Yet she does not lay in nests, but on the ground, and the eggs are deposited by the male in the nests of birds whose eggs they most resemble, and only one in each.

By-the-by, whilst in Santiago a quite severe quake occurred, but there were few casualties, only two people being killed. It was at night, and my bedroom being on the third floor of the only three-storey building in town, I continued to lie in bed, not indeed knowing what to do, and resigning myself to fate. I distinctly do not want to live in quaking countries!

The sensation produced on one by an earthquake is peculiar and different from all others. One is not so much alarmed as overawed; one feels so helpless, so insig- nificant; you know you can do nothing. What may happen next at any moment is beyond your ken; only when you realize that the disturbance has actually shaken these immense mountain masses and these boundless plains do you appreciate the forces that have caused it. The Krakatoa outbreak raised the water in our Thames four inches. A great Peruvian earthquake sent a tidal wave into the Red Sea.

Buenos Ayres is a city of some 1,200,000 people, half Italians (the working and go-ahead half) and half Spanish Americans. But there is also a very mixed popula- tion. There are many fine buildings and palatial residences, but the business streets are ridiculously narrow, save and except the Avenida de Mayo, which is one of the handsomest streets in the world. The new boulevards, the parks and race-tracks all deserve admiration. The hotels are not quite good enough--not even the palatial "Plaza." Prices, and indeed the cost of living, are quite as great as in New York. It was too hot to remain long, so I crossed to Montevideo, went all over the town; but beyond seeing (not meeting, alas!) one of the most beautiful girls I ever saw in my life, there was not much to interest. So, on the White Star Liner *Athenic*, I hastened to England. It may be remarked here that though Buenos Ayres and Santiago claim, and offer, wonderful displays of horsed carriages in their parks, if one watches them critically he will seldom see a really smart turn-out. The coachman's badly-made boots, or a strap out of place, or a buckle wanting, or blacking needed, all detract from the desirable London standard.

January 24th.--We entered beautiful Rio harbour. In the town the temperature was unbearable. The city is in the same transformation condition as Buenos Ayres; the streets are narrow, except the very handsome new Avenida Central. The esplanade on the bay is quite unequalled anywhere else. Surely a great future awaits Rio! A trip up Corcovada, a needle-like peak, some 2000 feet high, overlooking the bay, should not be missed. We sailed again for Teneriffe to coal, which gave us an opportunity to admire the grand peak and get some idea of the nature of the country. Thence home.

Perhaps a short note on the great historical personages of Central and South America may be of interest. Among these the greatest was Simon Bolivar, who with Miranda, the Apostle of Liberty, freed the Northern States of South America from Spanish dominion. It was Bolivar who in 1826 summoned the first International Peace Congress at Panama. San Martin, an equally great man, born in Argentina, freed the southern half of the Continent. Lopez, president in 1862 of Paraguay, has secured notoriety for having had the worst character in all American history. Petion, almost a pure negro, deserves also a prominent place. He was born in 1770, was a great, good and able man, and freed Haiti; he also assisted and advised Bolivar. May I also remind you here that Peru is the home of the Peruvian bark tree (cinchona) and the equally valuable coca plant, which gives us cocaine. Paraguay is the country of the yerba-mate, universally drunk there, supplanting tea, coffee, cocoa and coca. Like coca it has very stimulating qualities. El Dorado, the much-sought-for and fabulous, was vouched for by Juan Martinez, the chief of liars, who located it somewhere up the Orinoco River.

The Spaniards, and also the Portuguese, were wonderful colonizers and administrators. Just think what enormous territories their civilization influenced, and influenced for good. Certainly the torch of the Inquisition accompanied them; but even under that dreadful blight their colonies prospered and the conquered races became Iberianized, such was their masters' power of impressing their language, religion and manners on even barbarous tribes.

CHAPTER XIV
FIFTH TOUR ABROAD

California--Honolulu--Japan--China--Singapore--Burmah
--India--Ceylon--The End.

I hope these hasty notes, so hurriedly and scantily given, may have interested my readers enough to secure their company for one more globe-trot, which shall be rushed through in order to bring these reminiscences to a close.

A momentous event of 1910 was the death of King Edward VII., which threw everybody into deep mourning; and it seemed to me Englishwomen never looked so well as when dressed in black.

In the autumn I started for New York and Amarillo. Never before was I so impressed with the growth and improvement and possibilities of New York city, soon to be the most populous, wealthiest and greatest city the world has ever seen. The incomparable beauty of the American woods and forests in the fall again attracted me and afforded much pleasure.

From Amarillo I went on to San Francisco, stopping off to have yet one more sight of the Grand Canon of the Colorado River. San Francisco was now almost completely restored, and much on the old plan. Her Knob-hill palaces are gone, but her hotels are better and more palatial than ever.

November 22nd.--Sailed on a Japanese steamer for Yokohama, via Honolulu. These Japanese steamers are first-class, and noted for cleanliness and the politeness of the entire ship's company. We coaled at Honolulu and then proceeded. On approaching Yokohama we got a fine view of Fuji-San, the great national volcano, as it may be called, its perfect cone rising sheer from the low plain to a height of 12,700 feet. Fuji is at present quiescent; but Japan has some active volcanoes, and earthquakes are very frequent. My visit was at the least favourable time of the year, viz., in winter. The country should be seen in spring, during the cherry-blossom season, or in the autumn, when the tree foliage is almost more beautiful.

From Yokohama I went on to Tokio, formerly Jeddo, and now the capital. It is a large and busy city with some fine Government modern buildings. The palace, parks and temples form the sights. In the city proper as in all Japanese towns, the streets are very narrow and crowded with rickshaws, the only means of passenger conveyance. At the Anglo-Japanese dinner, given at my hotel, I had an opportunity of seeing Japanese men and women in full-dress attire, and to notice the extreme formalities of their greetings. A Japanese gentleman bows once, then again, and, as if he had forgotten something, after a short interval a third time. From Tokio I went to Kioto, formerly the residence of the Mikado, now purely a native city, with no modern buildings and still narrower streets; but it is the centre of the cloisonne, damascening and embroidery industries. Hotels in Japan are everywhere quite good. Here I visited the fencing and jiu-jitsu schools, which are attended by a large number of pupils, women as well as men. Also the geisha school, and saw girls taught dancing, music and tea ceremony. What perfectly delightful and charming little ladies Japanese girls of apparently all classes are. The smile of the geisha girl may be professional, but is very seductive and penetrating; so that the mere European man is soon a willing worshipper. The plump little waitresses in hotels and tea-houses, charmingly costumed, smiling as only they can smile, are incomparable. The Japanese, too, are the cleanest of all nations; the Chinese and Koreans among the dirtiest. They are extremely courteous as well as polite. A drunken man is hardly ever seen in Japan, a woman never. An angry word is hardly ever heard; indeed, the language has no "swear" words. All the people are artistic, even aesthetic. Arthur Diosy in his book declares that the Japanese are the most cheerful, peaceable, law-abiding and kindliest of all peoples. Up till the "Great Change," 1871, trade was considered unsuitable for, and degrading to, a gentleman. Women here, by-the-by, shave or have shaven the whole face, including the nose and ears, though not the eyebrows. How these Japs worship the beauties of Nature! Few of us might see much beauty in a purple cabbage; yet in my hotel purple cabbages were put in prominent places to decorate the dining-hall, and were really quite effective.

From Kioto I went to Nara, once the capital of the Empire, a pretty place with large park and interesting museum. A great religious festival was on, including a procession of men in ancient armour and costumes. There was also some horse-racing, which was quite comical. Apparently no European but myself was present. On travelling to Nara I passed through the tea district of Oji. The gardens are very beautiful and carefully tended. It was a great treat to me this first opportunity to see something of Japanese peasant life, and to admire the intensive and thorough cultivation. Not a foot of productive soil is wasted. The landscape of rice-fields, succeeded by tea-gardens, bamboo groves, up to the forest or brush-clad hills, and the very picturesque villages and farmhouses and rustic temples, form many a delightful picture. In the growing season the whole country must be very beautiful. Excellent trout and salmon fishing may then be had. The adopted national game for youths seems to be base-ball, and not cricket as in China.

Next I went to Kobe, via Osaka, the great manufacturing centre of the Empire. At Kobe took another Japanese steamer for Shanghai, calling at Moji, Shimonoseki and Nagasaki, and traversing the wonderfully beautiful inland Sea of Japan, a magnified, and quite as beautiful, Loch Lomond. This sea was dotted with innumerable fishing-boats. Indeed, Japan's sea-fisheries must be one of her most valuable assets. Moji harbour is a beautiful one, has an inlet and an outlet, but appears land-locked. On the mainland side is Shimonoseki, where Li Hung Chang signed the Peace Treaty with Japan, and where he was later wounded by an assassin. Nagasaki has also a fine harbour. From here I took a rickshaw ride over the hills to a lovely little summer coast-resort, passing through a most picturesque country.

Japan has, among many others, one particular curiosity in the shape of a domestic cock, possessing a tail as much as fifteen feet in length, and which tail receives its owner's, or rather its owner's owner's, most careful consideration. The unfortunate bird is kept in a very small wicker cage, so small that he can't turn round, the long tail feathers escaping through an aperture and drooping to the ground. Once a day the bird is taken out and allowed to exercise for a short time on a spotlessly clean floor-mat.

While in Japan I was told that her modern cultured men are satisfied with a simple work-a-day system of Ethics, priestly guidance being unnecessary, and they regard religion as being for the ignorant, superstitious or thoughtless. Thus they "emancipate their consciences from the conventional bonds of traditional religions."

It has been remarked that the Japanese will probably never again be such heroes, or at least will never be such reckless, fanatical fighters as they were in the late war, as civilization and property rights will make life more worth living and therefore preserving. The same might apply to the Fuzzy Wuzzies, to Cromwell's Ironsides, and to some extent our own Highlanders and others of a like fanatical tendency.

It had been my intention and hope to visit Korea, Port Arthur, Mukden and Peking; but was advised very strongly, on account of the extreme cold and almost Arctic conditions said to be prevailing in North China, not to go there. But at Shanghai I had better information, contradicting these reports and describing the weather as delightful at the capital. Shanghai has an immense river and ocean trade, and in the waterway are swung river gun-boats of all nations, as well as queer-looking Chinese armed junks, used in putting down piracy. I visited the city club, the country club, and the racecourse, and took a stroll at night through Soochow Road, among the native tea-houses, theatres, etc. Someone advised me to visit a town up the river on a certain day to witness the execution of some dozen river pirates and other criminals, a common occurrence; but such an attraction did not appeal to me.

In China, as in Japan and other countries, the German, often gross, selfish and vulgar, is ever present. But he is resourceful and determined, and threatens to push the placid Englishman to the wall.

Though the practice is not now permitted, Chinese women's bound and deformed feet are still to the stranger a constant source of wonder. It is said the custom arose in the desire of Court ladies to emulate the very tiny feet of a certain royal princess; but it is also suggested that the custom was instituted to stop the female gadding-about propensity!

Here in Shanghai I first observed edible swallow-nests in the market for sale. They did not look nice, but why should they not be so, knowing as we do that the young of swallows, unlike those of other birds, vent their ordure over the sides, so that the nests are not in any way defiled. Here I also learned that Pidgin, as in the expression "Pidgin" English, is John's attempt to pronounce "business."

From Shanghai to Soochow city, a typical Chinese walled town, still quite unmodernized, and no doubt the same as it was 2000 years ago. Tourists seldom enter it, and no European dwells within its walls, inside of which are crowded and jammed 500,000 souls. The main street was not more than six to eight *feet* wide, and so filled with such a jostling, busy crowd of people as surely could not be seen anywhere else on earth. Even rickshaws are not allowed to enter, there being no room for them. Progress can only be made on a donkey, and then with much shouting and discomfort. What a busy people the Chinese are! Some day they may people the earth. They seem to be even more intelligent than the Japanese, more honest and more industrious; and have an almost lovable disposition. And what giants they are compared to their neighbours!--the men from the north being especially so. I also went by narrow and vile-smelling streets to visit a celebrated leaning pagoda near Soochow, and on returning took the opportunity offered of inspecting with much interest a mandarin's rock-garden, purely Chinese and entirely different from Japanese similar retreats. In Shanghai I visited the original tea-house depicted on the well-known willow-pattern china ware.

January 1st.--Arrived at Hong-Kong and admired its splendid harbour and surroundings. This is one of the greatest seaports in the world, with an enormous trade. The whole island belongs to Great Britain; unlike Shanghai, where different nationalities merely have concessions. In the famous Happy Valley I had several days' golfing with a naval friend, and we played very badly. A trip up the river to Canton, the southern capital of China, an immense city with 2,000,000 population, was full of interest. Half the population seemingly live in boats.

What indefatigable workers the Chinese are. They seem to work all night and they seem to work all day. They are busy as ants. If one cannot find employment otherwise he will make it! Barring the beggars, there are no unemployed and no unemployables. What a mighty force they must become in the world's economy. We estimate China's population by millions, but forget to properly scale their energy and industry. What is the future of such a people to be! Yet they seem to be incapable of any general national movement: each is absorbed in his immediate work and contented to be so; so unlike the Japanese, with equal energy and industry, plus boundless ambition and patriotism.

The Chinaman's pigtail calls for explanation. The Manchus, on conquering China in 1644, decreed that all Chinese should shave the rest of the head but wear the pigtail. The Chinese would not submit to this; so the politic Manchu emperor further decreed that only loyal subjects might adopt the custom, criminals to be debarred. This ruse was so successful that now the Chinaman is even proud of his adornment, and little advantage is being taken of a recent relaxation of the decree.

Sailing for Singapore I was blessed with a cabin all to myself, and what a blessing it is! In all my travels I have been singularly fortunate in securing privacy in this way.

There is not much to interest in Singapore. It is one of the hottest places on earth, the same in winter and summer, purely tropical. It has, however, fine parks, streets and open places. The principal hotel is the "Raffles," which I should imagine is also the worst. The most notable feature of Singapore is the variety of "natives" domiciled there--Ceylonese, Burmese, Chinese, Japanese, Siamese, Hindoos and Malays. After leaving Singapore we looked in at Penang, where we had time to inspect a famous Chinese temple. An American Army General, D----, and his wife were among the passengers, and I found much pleasure in their company; indeed, we travelled thereafter much together in Burmah and India.

Rangoon, where we arrived next, is a large, well-laid-out city, as cosmopolitan as Singapore. The bazaars are well worth visiting, and the working of elephants in the great teak yards is one of the tourist's principal sights. But the great Shwe Dagon pagoda is of course the centre of interest, and indeed it is one of the most astonishing places of worship it has been my fortune to visit. The pagoda itself is of the typical bell shape, solidly built of brick, gilded from base to summit, and crowned with a golden Ti. The shrines, too, which surround and jostle it, hold the attention and wonder of the visitor. There are very many of these, mostly of graceful design, with delicate and intricate wood carvings and other decorations. The pagoda is the most venerated of all Buddhist places of worship, containing as it does not only the eight sacred hairs of Gautama, but also relics of the three Buddhas who preceded him. It is also from its great height, 370 feet (higher than St Paul's Cathedral), and graceful shape, extremely imposing and sublime.

From Rangoon I trained to Mandalay, on the Irawadi River, not a large town, but rich in historical associations, and famous for its Buddhist pagodas, such as The Incomparable and the Arakan; also the Queen's Golden Monastery. King Theebaw's palace remains much as it was, and well worth examination. The population here is almost purely Burmese; in fact you see the Burmese at their best, and the impression is always favourable. What brilliant but beautiful colours they affect in their head-clothes, jackets and silken gowns. They are a cheerful, light-hearted and good-natured people, lazy perhaps, but all apparently well enough to do. The boys and the young men play the national game of football, the ball, made simply of lightly-plaited bamboo strips, being kicked and tossed into the air with wonderful skill and activity, never being allowed to touch the ground. The way they can "take" the ball from behind, and with the heel or side of the foot toss it upwards and forwards, would be a revelation even to the Newcastle United. The women and girls have utmost freedom and are to be seen everywhere, often smoking enormous cigarettes: merry and careless, but always well, and often charmingly, dressed.

A fine view, and good idea, of the great Irawadi River may be obtained from Mandalay; but time was pressing, so I railed back to Rangoon instead of making the river trip, which my friends, the D----s, did.

The steamer to Calcutta was unusually crowded, but I was again fortunate enough to secure the use of the pilot's cabin all to myself. The Hugli River was familiar even after thirty-four years' absence, and in Calcutta I noticed little change. The hotels, including the Grand and Continental, are quite unworthy of the city, only the very old and well-known Great Eastern approaching the first-class character. Calcutta was getting hot, so I at once went on to Darjeeling, hoping to get a view of what my eyes had ever longed to see--the glorious high peaks of the Himalayas, and the roof of the world. After a few hours' run through the celebrated Terai jungle, the haunt, and probably final sanctuary, of the big game of India, the track ascends rapidly and picturesquely through the tea district of Kangra, and arrives at Darjeeling, elevation 7500 feet, the summer home of the Bengal Government and the merchant princes of Calcutta and elsewhere. I had been forewarned that the chances of seeing the high peaks at this time of the year were extremely slim; but my experience and disappointment in connection with Korea and Peking taught me to disregard such warnings; and, as it turned out, I was rewarded with a perfect day and magnificent views of Mounts Kinchinjunga and Everest, and all the other majestic heights; seen, too, in all their phases of cloud and mist, of perfectly clear blue sky, and of sunrise and sunset effects. It was indeed a most satisfying and absorbing twenty-four hours' visit, as I had also time, under the guidance of an official friend, to visit the picturesque weekly market or bazaar, where natives from Sikkim, Nepal, Butan and Tibet may be seen in all their dirt and strangeness. Also the quite beautiful Botanic Gardens, the Club House, the prayer-wheels, etc. More than that, I was privileged to pay my respects to the Dalai Lama, who had but recently left his kingdom and taken refuge here. The acknowledged spiritual head of the Buddhists of Mongolia and China is a young man with a dreamy, absorbed expression of countenance, perhaps not of much intellectuality, but who is approachable even to the merely curious. My friend and kind cicerone was Commissioner of the Bengal police, and was extremely busy laying guards along the railroad and taking all other necessary precautions for the safety of the German Imperial Crown Prince during his projected visit to Darjeeling, a visit ultimately abandoned. I can imagine his chagrin at the waste of all his labours, expense to the Indian Government, etc. etc., due to the caprice of this apparently frivolous and not quite courteous young hopeful. Indeed, the Crown Prince, though a popular young fellow enough, was the source of trouble and tribulation to his hosts, breaking conventions and scandalizing Society by his disregard of its usages.

Returning to Calcutta I thence took train to Agra via Allahabad, purposely, on account of the great discomfort and poor hotel accommodation due to the large tourist traffic, avoiding Lucknow, Benares and Cawnpore. At Allahabad the Aga Khan, temporal head of the Mohammedans of India, and a man of great authority and influence, joined our train, and part of the way I was lucky enough to be in his company and had an opportunity of speaking with him. In appearance he is a Turk, quite European in dress, and seems capable, energetic, sociable and agreeable. At every stopping-place he received an ovation, crowds of his Mussulman supporters and friends, among them apparently being chiefs and rajahs and other men of high degree, greeting him with much enthusiasm, which enthusiasm I learned was aroused by His Highness' endeavour towards the raising of the status of the Mohammedan College of Aligarh to that of a university.

I should say here that, on Indian railways, the first-class carriages are divided into compartments, containing each four beds, but in which it is customary to put only two passengers, at least during sleeping hours, and unless an unusual crowd requires otherwise.

It was also on this train I made the acquaintance of a gentleman on his way to visit the Maharaja of Gwalior, and who was kind enough to ask me to accompany

him. I told him that if he would secure me an invitation from the Maharaja I would
be only too pleased to do so. Gwalior was a place on my itinerary anyway; to go there
as a guest would secure me many advantages not attainable by the ordinary tourist.
My friend said he would see the Maharaja at once and have my visit arranged for. A
few days afterwards I received advice that it had been done, so on arrival at Gwalior
I was met by one of the State carriages and conveyed to the Guest House, formerly
the zenana, close to the palace, a very beautiful and handsome building, where an
excellent staff of servants, capital meals, choice liquors and cigars, were at our free
disposal. His Highness does not eat with his guests, but they are all put up in this
building; and during big shoots, durbars, or festive occasions, the house is always
full. At the time of my visit the few guests included two Scotch manufacturers, who
had just effected large sales of machinery to the Maharaja, the one securing from
him an order worth L60,000 for steam-breaking ploughs, the other an order of some
L20,000 for pumping appliances. The Maharaja is a thoroughly progressive man, has
an enormous revenue, and devotes a large part of it to the bringing into cultivation
tracts of hitherto unbroken and unoccupied land, which no doubt will eventually
increase his revenue and provide homesteads for his people. Sindia, as his name is, is
a keen soldier, a keen sportsman, and most loyal to the British Raj. He moves about
freely, wearing a rough tweed suit, is busy and occupied all day long, and though he
has ministers and officials of all degrees, and keeps great state on occasion, his army
numbering some 5000 men, he finds time to superintend the various departments
of his Government, and to administer his State with a thoroughness uncommon
among Indian potentates. The new palace is very beautiful and furnished in European manner, apparently quite regardless of expense. The crystal chandeliers in the
reception-rooms are magnificent, and must alone represent fabulous sums. Near
by the palace are a number of lions, now kept in proper cages, but I must say from
the smell and filth not under very sanitary conditions. These lions he had imported
from abroad and turned loose to furnish sport to his shooting friends; but they killed
so many of the peasantry that they had to be recaptured and confined. The town of
Lashkar, the State capital city, being reported full of plague, I was naturally careful
in passing through. Nothing in it calls for comment, however. Gwalior Fort, on a
high rocky plateau, has much historic interest. In it are the ancient palaces, still in
fair condition but long ago abandoned, certain Jain temples covered with bas-relief

carvings, tanks and many old ruins. The entrance is handsome and impressive. My friend and myself were supplied with an elephant, so we rode all over the immense fort, now almost silent, having only a small guard and a few other occupants. Altogether I enjoyed the visit very much, and after three or four days' stay returned to Agra. Everyone knows Agra, with its heavenly Taj-Mahal, its great fortress, its pearl mosque, its beautiful halls of audience and its palaces. It is truly sad to know that one of our former Governor-Generals actually proposed to tear down the Taj-Mahal so that he could use the marble for other purposes! Among these delights of architecture one could wander for days, ever with an unquenched greed for the charm of their beauties. One sees marbled trellis-work of exquisite design and execution, and inlaid flower wreaths and scrolls of red cornelian and precious stone, as beautiful in colour as graceful in form. Agra's cantonment avenues and parks are kept in excellent order. The temperature at the time of my visit was delightfully cool, and the hotel the best I had yet found in India. Fatepur Sikri, a royal city built by Akbar, only to be abandoned by him again, is near Agra, and possesses enough deserted palaces, mosques and other beautiful buildings to make it well worth a visit.

There is, for instance, the great mosque, rival to the Taj-Mahal, the inside of which is entirely overlaid with mother-of-pearl.

From Agra I went to Delhi, India's imperial city. In and around it are innumerable palaces, mosques, tombs and forts, each and all worthy of careful inspection; but I will only mention the Jama Musjid; inside the fort the Diwan-i-Am, wherein formerly stood the famous peacock throne; and the Diwan-i-Kas, at either end of which, over the outer arches, is the famous Persian inscription, "If Heaven can be on the face of the earth it is this! Oh, it is this! Oh, it is this!" In the city itself is the famous street called Chandni Chauk. North of the city is a district where the principal incidents of the siege took place, and there also is the plain devoted to imperial durbars and assemblages. South of the city are many celebrated tombs, such as those of Emperor Humayun, and of Tughlak; and the majestic Kutab Minar. Mutiny recollections of course enormously add to one's interest in Delhi, and many days may be agreeably passed in company with her other historic, tragic and romantic associations. At the time of my visit preparations were already beginning for the great Coronation Durbar to be held next winter. Most hotels and private houses have already been leased. What the general public will do for accommodation I do not know. One will almost necessarily, like the King, have to go under canvas. The Circuit House will only be used by His Majesty should bad weather prevail. The native rulers of every grade are going to make such a display of Oriental magnificence as was never seen before. To many it will be their ruin, or at least a serious crippling of their resources; but it is a chance for display that does not often occur and they seem determined to make the most of it.

Here at Delhi the General and myself again joined forces, he and his wife having visited Lucknow and Cawnpore. We took train direct to Peshawar, via Rawal Pindi and Lahore. I never knew anyone who enjoyed foreign travel so much as my American friend. He was in a constant state of delight, finding interest and pleasure in small matters that never even attracted my attention, though as a rule my faculty for observation is by no means obtuse. In Burmah the bright-hued cupras of the natives filled him with intense joy, and the presence of some closely-screened native ladies on a ferryboat so held his gaze that his wife (and I suspect they were not long married) must have felt pangs of jealousy. But he was a keen soldier, and had frequently represented his country at the German and other manoeuvres, and had been Adjutant-General at the inauguration of President Roosevelt, a very honourable position indeed. So he was intensely interested in old forts and battlefields, and his enthusiasm while in Peshawar and the Khaiber Pass was boundless. More than that he was a strong Anglo-Phile, and amused me by his disparaging criticism on how his own Government did things in the Philippines and elsewhere, compared with what he saw in India and other British possessions. Peshawar is a very delightful place, or so at least it appeared to me. We lodged in a capital though small hotel. The climate was then very agreeable; the cantonment gardens and avenues are a paradise of beauty, at least compared with the surrounding dry and semi-barren country. In the native city one mixed with new races of people, Afghans and Asians, and picturesque and fierce-looking tribesmen from the hills. Also an immense number of camels, the only means of traffic communication with western and northern native states.

But before arriving at Peshawar one must not forget to mention the magnificent view obtained from the car windows of the glorious range of Cashmere Snowy Mountains, showing peaks of 20,000 to 25,000 feet elevation; nor the crossing by a fortified railway bridge of the historic Indus River, near Attock, at the very spot where the Greek Alexander entered India on his campaign of conquest A mile above this point the Kabul River joins the Indus. Here too is a romantic-looking town and fortress built by the Emperor Akbar, still unimpaired and in occupation by British troops. The approaches to the bridge and fort are strongly guarded, emplacements for guns being noticeable at every vantage point on the surrounding hills, while ancient round towers and other fortifications tell of the troublous times and martial deeds this important position has been witness to.

For our visit to the Khaiber Pass General Nixon, Commandant at Peshawar, put a carriage at our disposal, in which we drove as far as Jamrud, the isolated fort so often pictured in our illustrated papers, where we exchanged into tongas, in which to complete the journey through the pass as far as Ali Musjid. The pass is now patrolled by the Afridi Rifles, a corps composed of Afridi tribesmen commanded by British officers. At frequent intervals along the route these Afridi sentinels can be seen standing on silent guard on all commanding points of the hills. One sees numerous Afridi hamlets, though what the occupants find to support themselves with it is difficult to understand. A good carriage road continues all the way, in places steep enough and tortuous, as the rough broken nature of the country necessitates. By another road or trail, paralleling our own, a continuous string of camel caravans proceeds in single file at a leisurely gait, the animals loaded with merchandise for the Kabul market and others in Central Asia. It is a rough, desolate and uninteresting country, yet grand and beautiful in its way, and one is at once struck with the difficulties to be encountered by troops endeavouring to force their way through, commanded as the pass is at every turn by positions so admirably suited for guerrilla warfare and delightful possibilities for an enemy with sniping propensities. At Ali Musjid the camel and carriage tracks come together. Here at this little mosque was the point beyond which we were not allowed to proceed; so after a most interesting visit we returned to Peshawar. We were most fortunate in the weather, as the strong wind which always blows down the pass is in winter time generally excessively cold. At Peshawar I bade good-bye to my most agreeable American friends, the General being keen on visiting Quetta; whither, had it not been so much out of my own proposed line of travel, I would gladly have accompanied him. So my next move was back to Delhi, and thence by train via Jeypore to Udaipur, one of the most delightfully picturesque and interesting of all Indian native capitals. There is a tiny little hotel at Udaipur, outside the walls, showing that visiting tourists are few and far between. The Maharana holds by his old and established customs, and has none of the modern spirit shown by such princes as Sindia, the Nizam, and certain other native chiefs. He has, however, gone so far as to furnish his new palace in a most gorgeous manner, the chairs, tables, mirror frames, bedsteads seen in the State apartments being composed of crystal glass. The show attraction of the palace, in the eyes of the attendants, who were ever at one's beck and call, was a Teddy dog with wagging head, which miracle of miracles one seemed to be expected to properly marvel at. The old palace, adjoining the new, is a much finer building, being mostly of marble, and is purely Oriental in its stairways, doorways, closets, balconies and delightful roof-gardens, as one's preconceived notions expect an Eastern potentate's palace to be. The new palace showed no sign of occupancy, and I imagined the Maharana, then absent, really favours the older building, and small blame to him! Around in various places the State elephants are stabled, or rather chained, in the open air, and looked after by their numerous attendants. In the grand court in front were several of these animals, and a myriad of pigeons, protected by their sanctity, flew about in clouds, or perched on the projections of the palace walls. From a boat on the large and lovely lake, on whose very edge the commanding palace stands, a beautiful view is obtained. On islands in the lake two delightful little summer palaces are built, of white marble and luxuriously furnished within. Elephants were bathing themselves at the water's edge, and the roar of caged lions was heard from the neighbouring royal garden. Pea-fowl perched on the marble colonnade, and pigeons were circling and sailing in the glorious sunshine. What a sight! especially when evening drew in, and the setting sun lighted up the graceful cupolas and domes, and threw shadows round the towers and battlements, the whole reflected in the glassy surface of the water. At one place near by the wild pigs approached to be fed and some grand old fellows may be seen amongst them.

It is still the custom of nearly all men here above the rank of coolie to carry swords or other weapons. For are these Rajputs not of a proud and warlike race, as may be seen by their bearing; and is not their Maharana of the longest lineage in India, and the highest in rank of all the Rajput princes? A few miles from the capital is Chitorgarh. Here I saw the wonderful old fortress, with its noble entrance gate, and the ancient town of Chitor, once the capital of Mewar. Also the two imposing

PALACE OF MAJARANA OF UDAIPUR.

towers of Fame and Victory. Throughout the state one is struck by the great number of wild pea-fowl picking their way through the stubble just as pheasants do. The flesh of pea-fowl, which I have tasted, is excellent eating, surpassing that of the pheasant. One also sees numbers of a large grey, long-tailed monkey, which seem to preferably attach themselves to old and ruined temples or tombs. From here, Chitorgarh, I next took train to Bombay, passing through Rutlam, a great poppy-producing centre. At Baroda I received into my compartment the brother of the late Gaikwar (uncle of the present?). It had often occurred to me before to wonder how the high-class natives travel on the railways. Never had I yet seen a native enter a first-class compartment where there happened to be any Europeans. In this instance, at Baroda, I had noticed a man, apparently of consequence, judging by his attendants, evidently wanting to travel by this train. Soon one of the party approached, and almost humbly, it seemed more than politely, asked if I would have no objection to the company of the brother of the Gaikwar. Of course I said I could have no objection, and so we travelled together to Bombay. But what is the feeling between the two races that keeps them thus apart?

Bombay surprised me more by the delightfully cold breeze then blowing than by anything else. I took a drive over Malabar Hill and saw the Parsee Towers of Silence, as they are popularly called. The immense Taj Hotel, where I stayed one night, by no means justifies its pretensions. Indeed, it is one of the poorest or worst in all India. Next day I started out for Hyderabad, and had a long, hot, slow twenty-four hours' journey; the principal crop noticed being to me the familiar Kafir corn. Yes, it was very hot and dusty. As usual, the train was packed with natives, but myself seemed to be the only European on board. Arrived at Hyderabad, I at once drove over to Secunderabad, a very large British cantonment and station. From here, missing the friends I had come to see, and there being nothing to specially interest otherwise, I again took train to Madras. A letter of introduction in my pocket to the Nizam's Prime Minister might have been useful in seeing the city had I presented it, but pressure of time induced me to push on; nor did I stop in Madras longer than to allow of a drive round the city, the heat being very great. Indeed, I was getting very tired of such hurried travel and sight-seeing, and was longing for a week's rest and quietude in the cool and pleasant highlands of Ceylon. My health also was now giving me some concern; so on again to Madura, *en route* to Tuticorin, from whence a steamer would take me across to the land of spicy breezes. Madura has a wonderful old temple of immense size, surrounded by gopuras of pyramidal form, in whose construction huge stones of enormous dimensions were utilized; the temple also has much fine carving, etc. The old palace is of great beauty and interest.

Colombo was, as usual, uncomfortably warm; only on the seashore at Galle Face could one get relief, and Galle Face with its excellent hotel is certainly a very delightful place. I did not stay in Colombo, but at once took train to visit Anauradapura and the dead cities of Ceylon. Here was the heart of a district ten miles in diameter, practically covered by the site and remains of the ancient city, which in its prime, about the beginning of the Christian era, ranked with Babylon and Nineveh in its dimensions, population and magnificence. Its walls included an area of 260 square miles. Among its ruins the most notable are the dagobas (pagodas), some of such enormous size that the number of bricks used in their construction baffles conception. One of the dagobas has a diameter of 327 feet and a height of 270. It is solidly built of bricks, and contains material enough to build a complete modern town of 50,000 people. These Buddhist dagobas of Ceylon have the bell-shape form, and serve the same purpose as the Shwe Dagon in Rangoon, viz., to shelter relics of the Buddhas. Close by, within the walls of a Buddhist temple, or monastery, still grows the famous Bo or Pipal tree, the oldest living historical tree in the world, brought here 250 B.C. from Buddh Gaya in India. Only a fragment of the original main trunk now exists, the various offshoots growing vigorously in the surrounding compound, all still guarded and attended by the priests as lovingly as when done 2200 years ago. At Anauradapura is a quite charming little Rest House, shaded and surrounded by beautiful tropical trees of great variety.

From here I went to Kandy, the former capital of the native kings of that name. In the fourteenth century a temple was erected here to contain a tooth of Buddha and other relics. Later, the temple was sacked and the sacred tooth destroyed, but another to which was given similar attributes was put in its place. Kandy is a pretty spot, with a good hotel and agreeable climate, its elevation being 1800 feet above sea-level. Near by is Paradenia and the beautiful Botanical Gardens, in which it is a perfect delight to wander.

We had already passed through a most lovely and picturesque country; but the grandest and most impressive scenery of Ceylon lies between Kandy and Newara

Elia. Tea-gardens extend everywhere, and the cosy, neat-looking bungalows of the planters have a most attractive appearance. Newara Elia stands very high, some 7000 feet. Its vegetation is that of a temperate climate, and in the winter months the climate itself is ideal. The bracing atmosphere suggests golf and all other kinds of sport, and golfing there is of the very best kind. There is an excellent hotel, though I myself put up at the Hill Club. All Ceylon is beautiful, the roads are good, and many delightful excursions can be made. I do not think I ever saw a more beautiful country. But the sailing date draws near, so I must hurry down again to Colombo, and thus practically complete my second tour round the world. A P. & O. steamer brought us to Aden, the canal, Messina and Marseilles. We enjoyed lovely cool and calm weather all the way till near the end, when off the "balmy" coast of the Riviera we encountered bitter cold winds and stormy seas. And so through France to England, to the best country of them all, even though it be the land of coined currency bearing no testimony to its value; where registered letters may be receipted for by others than the addressee; and where butcher meat is freely exposed in the shops, and even outside, to all the filth that flies--my last fling at the dear old country.

Someone has asked me which was the most beautiful place I had ever seen? It was impossible to answer. The whole world is beautiful! The barren desert, the boundless ocean, the mountain region and the flat country, even these monotonous Staked Plains of New Mexico, under storm or sunshine, all equally compel us to admiration and wonderment.

In closing this somewhat higgledy-piggledy narrative, let me once more express my hope that readers will have found in it some entertainment, perhaps instruction, and possibly amusement.

APPENDIX

Note I. --An outcry against Mormonism has been raised lately in this country. It is its polygamous character that has been attacked. But does polygamy deserve all that is said about it? It is not immoral and should not be criminal. Compare it with the very vicious modern custom of restricted families, which is immoral and should be criminal. Where is our population going to come from? The Chinese, Japanese, Indians and negroes are swarming all over the earth; while our race is almost stagnant, yet owning and claiming continents and islands practically unpeopled. Some day, possibly, polygamy will have to be permitted, even by the most civilized of nations.

Note II. --In this present year there is much writing and much talking about arbitration treaties and preferential tariffs. A general arbitration on *all* matters between the United States and Great Britain is probably quite impracticable. Preferential tariff within the Empire would be highly advantageous to the Mother Country. If so, let us go for it while the opportunity offers. But it does seem to me there is a much-mistaken idea prevalent at home as to the loyalty of the Colonies and Dominions. One travels for information and should be allowed to give his conclusions. What holds these offshoots to the mother stem? Loyalty? I think not. Simply the realization that they are not (not yet) strong enough to stand alone: and it is the opinion of many that, as soon as they are, loyalty will be thrown to the winds; and naturally! (Since the above was written has it not been abundantly verified?) There is also even a belief (the wish being father to the thought) that the United States of America have a sentimental feeling for the Old Country; and one frequently hears the platform or banquet stock phrase, "Blood is thicker than water." It would be well if our people were enlightened with the truth. After twenty-five years' residence in the United States I will dare to say that the two nations are entirely foreign and antagonistic one to another. And it is a fortunate thing that between them few "Questions" remain to be arbitrated either by pen or sword. The two peoples do not understand one another, and do not try to. The ordinary English traveller does not meet or mix with the real American people, who are rapidly developing a civilization entirely their own, in social customs, in civil government, and even in fashions of dress.

Note III. --Might a just comparison not be drawn between these "dogies" and the type of men we now recruit for our standing Army? Are they not dogies? Is it not a fact that many of them never had a square meal in their lives! At least they look like it. But when taken up, if not while yet babies at least when they are still at a critical age of development, say eighteen years, and fed substantially and satisfyingly, as is now done in the Army, what an almost miraculous physical change takes place! And not only physical, but mental and moral, due to the influence of discipline and athletic exercises. If such be the effect on our few annual recruits, why not submit the whole young manhood of the nation to such beneficial conditions by the introduction of compulsory national military service? And not only that! Is not the private soldier of this country, alone of all others, refused admission to certain places of entertainment open to the public? Why? Because he is a hireling. Because no man of character or independence will adopt such a calling. He would degrade himself by doing so. But make the service compulsory to all men, and at once the calling becomes an honourable one. Can it be imagined for a moment that any of our raw recruits enter the service from a love for King and country? No; they sell their birthright for a red coat and a pittance, renounce their independence and stultify the natural ambition that should stimulate every man worthy of the name.

Though our men do not have the initiative and self-resource of the Americans, still they are the smartest and best-set-up troops in the world. Many of them are of splendid physique and look like they could go anywhere and do anything. The whole world *was* open to them; yet here they still are in the ranks, dummies and automatons, devoid of ambition and self-assertiveness.

Only national service will rid us of the army of unemployables. It will develop them physically and mentally, and make men of them such as our Colonies will be glad and proud to admit to citizenship.

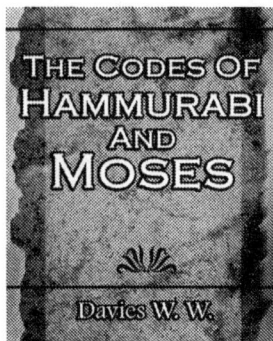

The Codes Of Hammurabi And Moses
W. W. Davies

QTY

The discovery of the Hammurabi Code is one of the greatest achievements of archaeology, and is of paramount interest, not only to the student of the Bible, but also to all those interested in ancient history...

Religion   ISBN: *1-59462-338-4*   **Pages:132**
MSRP $12.95

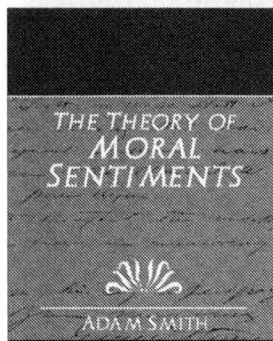

The Theory of Moral Sentiments
Adam Smith

QTY

This work from 1749. contains original theories of conscience amd moral judgment and it is the foundation for systemof morals.

Philosophy ISBN: *1-59462-777-0*   **Pages:536**
MSRP $19.95

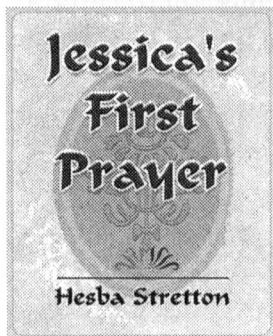

Jessica's First Prayer
Hesba Stretton

QTY

In a screened and secluded corner of one of the many railway-bridges which span the streets of London there could be seen a few years ago, from five o'clock every morning until half past eight, a tidily set-out coffee-stall, consisting of a trestle and board, upon which stood two large tin cans, with a small fire of charcoal burning under each so as to keep the coffee boiling during the early hours of the morning when the work-people were thronging into the city on their way to their daily toil...

Childrens   ISBN: *1-59462-373-2*   **Pages:84**
MSRP $9.95

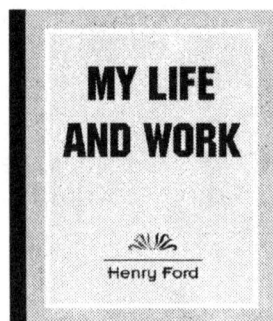

My Life and Work
Henry Ford

QTY

Henry Ford revolutionized the world with his implementation of mass production for the Model T automobile. Gain valuable business insight into his life and work with his own auto-biography... "We have only started on our development of our country we have not as yet, with all our talk of wonderful progress, done more than scratch the surface. The progress has been wonderful enough but..."

Biographies/ ISBN: *1-59462-198-5*   **Pages:300**
MSRP $21.95

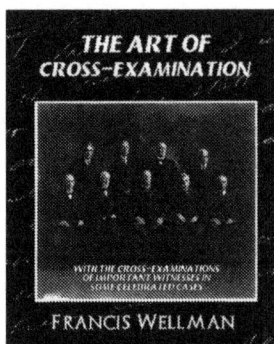

The Art of Cross-Examination
Francis Wellman

QTY

I presume it is the experience of every author, after his first book is published upon an important subject, to be almost overwhelmed with a wealth of ideas and illustrations which could readily have been included in his book, and which to his own mind, at least, seem to make a second edition inevitable. Such certainly was the case with me; and when the first edition had reached its sixth impression in five months, I rejoiced to learn that it seemed to my publishers that the book had met with a sufficiently favorable reception to justify a second and considerably enlarged edition. ..

Pages:412

Reference   ISBN: *1-59462-647-2*   *MSRP $19.95*

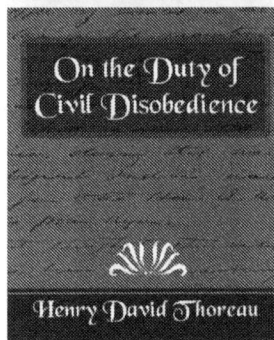

On the Duty of Civil Disobedience
Henry David Thoreau

QTY

Thoreau wrote his famous essay, On the Duty of Civil Disobedience, as a protest against an unjust but popular war and the immoral but popular institution of slave-owning. He did more than write—he declined to pay his taxes,   and was hauled off to gaol in consequence. Who can say how much this refusal of his hastened the end of the war and of slavery ?

Law   ISBN: *1-59462-747-9*   **Pages:48**
MSRP $7.45

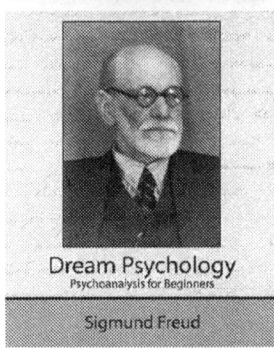

Dream Psychology Psychoanalysis for Beginners
Sigmund Freud

QTY

Sigmund Freud, born Sigismund Schlomo Freud (May 6, 1856 - September 23, 1939), was a Jewish-Austrian neurologist and psychiatrist who co-founded the psychoanalytic school of psychology. Freud is best known for his theories of the unconscious mind, especially involving the mechanism of repression; his redefinition of sexual desire as mobile and directed towards a wide variety of objects; and his therapeutic techniques, especially his understanding of transference in the therapeutic relationship and the presumed value of dreams as sources of insight into unconscious desires.

Pages:196

Psychology   ISBN: *1-59462-905-6*   *MSRP $15.45*

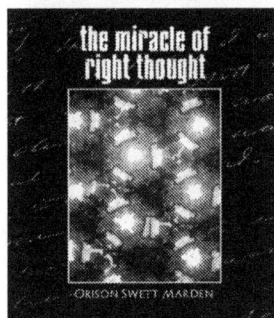

The Miracle of Right Thought
Orison Swett Marden

QTY

Believe with all of your heart that you will do what you were made to do. When the mind has once formed the habit of holding cheerful, happy, prosperous pictures, it will not be easy to form the opposite habit. It does not matter how improbable or how far away this realization may see, or how dark the prospects may be, if we visualize them as best we can, as vividly as possible, hold tenaciously to them and vigorously struggle to attain them, they will gradually become actualized, realized in the life. But a desire, a longing without endeavor, a yearning abandoned or held indifferently will vanish without realization.

Pages:360

Self Help   ISBN: *1-59462-644-8*   *MSRP $25.45*

QTY

The Rosicrucian Cosmo-Conception Mystic Christianity *by Max Heindel*   ISBN: 1-59462-188-8   **$38.95**
The Rosicrucian Cosmo-conception is not dogmatic, neither does it appeal to any other authority than the reason of the student. It is: not controversial, but is: sent forth in the, hope that it may help to clear..   New Age/Religion Pages 646

Abandonment To Divine Providence *by Jean-Pierre de Caussade*   ISBN: 1-59462-228-0   **$25.95**
"The Rev. Jean Pierre de Caussade was one of the most remarkable spiritual writers of the Society of Jesus in France in the 18th Century. His death took place at Toulouse in 1751. His works have gone through many editions and have been republished...   Inspirational/Religion Pages 400

Mental Chemistry *by Charles Haanel*   ISBN: 1-59462-192-6   **$23.95**
Mental Chemistry allows the change of material conditions by combining and appropriately utilizing the power of the mind. Much like applied chemistry creates something new and unique out of careful combinations of chemicals the mastery of mental chemistry...   New Age Pages 354

The Letters of Robert Browning and Elizabeth Barret Barrett 1845-1846 vol II   ISBN: 1-59462-193-4   **$35.95**
by Robert Browning and *Elizabeth Barrett*   Biographies Pages 596

Gleanings In Genesis (volume I) *by Arthur W. Pink*   ISBN: 1-59462-130-6   **$27.45**
Appropriately has Genesis been termed "the seed plot of the Bible" for in it we have, in germ form, almost all of the great doctrines which are afterwards fully developed in the books of Scripture which follow...   Religion/Inspirational Pages 420

The Master Key *by L. W. de Laurence*   ISBN: 1-59462-001-6   **$30.95**
In no branch of human knowledge has there been a more lively increase of the spirit of research during the past few years than in the study of Psychology, Concentration and Mental Discipline. The requests for authentic lessons in Thought Control, Mental Discipline and...   New Age/Business Pages 422

The Lesser Key Of Solomon Goetia *by L. W. de Laurence*   ISBN: 1-59462-092-X   **$9.95**
This translation of the first book of the "Lemegton" which is now for the first time made accessible to students of Talismanic Magic was done, after careful collation and edition, from numerous Ancient Manuscripts in Hebrew, Latin, and French...   New Age/Occult Pages 92

Rubaiyat Of Omar Khayyam *by Edward Fitzgerald*   ISBN:1-59462-332-5   **$13.95**
Edward Fitzgerald, whom the world has already learned, in spite of his own efforts to remain within the shadow of anonymity, to look upon as one of the rarest poets of the century, was born at Bredfield, in Suffolk, on the 31st of March, 1809. He was the third son of John Purcell...   Music Pages 172

Ancient Law *by Henry Maine*   ISBN: 1-59462-128-4   **$29.95**
The chief object of the following pages is to indicate some of the earliest ideas of mankind, as they are reflected in Ancient Law, and to point out the relation of those ideas to modern thought.   Religion/History Pages 452

Far-Away Stories *by William J. Locke*   ISBN: 1-59462-129-2   **$19.45**
"Good wine needs no bush, but a collection of mixed vintages does. And this book is just such a collection. Some of the stories I do not want to remain buried for ever in the museum files of dead magazine-numbers an author's not unpardonable vanity..."   Fiction Pages 272

Life of David Crockett *by David Crockett*   ISBN: 1-59462-250-7   **$27.45**
"Colonel David Crockett was one of the most remarkable men of the times in which he lived. Born in humble life, but gifted with a strong will, an indomitable courage, and unremitting perseverance...   Biographies/New Age Pages 424

Lip-Reading *by Edward Nitchie*   ISBN: 1-59462-206-X   **$25.95**
Edward B. Nitchie, founder of the New York School for the Hard of Hearing, now the Nitchie School of Lip-Reading, Inc, wrote "LIP-READING Principles and Practice". The development and perfecting of this meritorious work on lip-reading was an undertaking...   How-to Pages 400

A Handbook of Suggestive Therapeutics, Applied Hypnotism, Psychic Science   ISBN: 1-59462-214-0   **$24.95**
by Henry Munro   Health/New Age/Health/Self-help Pages 376

A Doll's House: and Two Other Plays *by Henrik Ibsen*   ISBN: 1-59462-112-8   **$19.95**
Henrik Ibsen created this classic when in revolutionary 1848 Rome. Introducing some striking concepts in playwriting for the realist genre, this play has been studied the world over.   Fiction/Classics/Plays 308

The Light of Asia *by sir Edwin Arnold*   ISBN: 1-59462-204-3   **$13.95**
In this poetic masterpiece, Edwin Arnold describes the life and teachings of Buddha. The man who was to become known as Buddha to the world was born as Prince Gautama of India but he rejected the worldly riches and abandoned the reigns of power when...   Religion/History/Biographies Pages 170

The Complete Works of Guy de Maupassant *by Guy de Maupassant*   ISBN: 1-59462-157-8   **$16.95**
"For days and days, nights and nights, I had dreamed of that first kiss which was to consecrate our engagement, and I knew not on what spot I should put my lips..."   Fiction/Classics Pages 240

The Art of Cross-Examination *by Francis L. Wellman*   ISBN: 1-59462-309-0   **$26.95**
Written by a renowned trial lawyer, Wellman imparts his experience and uses case studies to explain how to use psychology to extract desired information through questioning.   How-to/Science/Reference Pages 408

Answered or Unanswered? *by Louisa Vaughan*   ISBN: 1-59462-248-5   **$10.95**
Miracles of Faith in China   Religion Pages 112

The Edinburgh Lectures on Mental Science (1909) *by Thomas*   ISBN: 1-59462-008-3   **$11.95**
This book contains the substance of a course of lectures recently given by the writer in the Queen Street Hall, Edinburgh. Its purpose is to indicate the Natural Principles governing the relation between Mental Action and Material Conditions...   New Age/Psychology Pages 148

Ayesha *by H. Rider Haggard*   ISBN: 1-59462-301-5   **$24.95**
Verily and indeed it is the unexpected that happens! Probably if there was one person upon the earth from whom the Editor of this, and of a certain previous history, did not expect to hear again...   Classics Pages 380

Ayala's Angel *by Anthony Trollope*   ISBN: 1-59462-352-X   **$29.95**
The two girls were both pretty, but Lucy who was twenty-one who supposed to be simple and comparatively unattractive, whereas Ayala was credited, as her Bombwhat romantic name might show, with poetic charm and a taste for romance. Ayala when her father died was nineteen...   Fiction Pages 484

The American Commonwealth *by James Bryce*   ISBN: 1-59462-286-8   **$34.45**
An interpretation of American democratic political theory. It examines political mechanics and society from the perspective of Scotsman James Bryce   Politics Pages 572

Stories of the Pilgrims *by Margaret P. Pumphrey*   ISBN: 1-59462-116-0   **$17.95**
This book explores pilgrims religious oppression in England as well as their escape to Holland and eventual crossing to America on the Mayflower, and their early days in New England...   History Pages 268

www.bookjungle.com *email: sales@bookjungle.com fax: 630-214-0564 mail: Book Jungle PO Box 2226 Champaign, IL 61825*

QTY

The Fasting Cure *by Sinclair Upton*   ISBN: *1-59462-222-1*   **$13.95**

In the Cosmopolitan Magazine for May, 1910, and in the Contemporary Review (London) for April, 1910, I published an article dealing with my experiences in fasting. I have written a great many magazine articles, but never one which attracted so much attention... New Age/Self Help/Health Pages 164

Hebrew Astrology *by Sepharial*   ISBN: *1-59462-308-2*   **$13.45**

In these days of advanced thinking it is a matter of common observation that we have left many of the old landmarks behind and that we are now pressing forward to greater heights and to a wider horizon than that which represented the mind-content of our progenitors... Astrology Pages 144

Thought Vibration or The Law of Attraction in the Thought World   ISBN: *1-59462-127-6*   **$12.95**

by William Walker Atkinson   *Psychology/Religion Pages 144*

Optimism *by Helen Keller*   ISBN: *1-59462-108-X*   **$15.95**

Helen Keller was blind, deaf, and mute since 19 months old, yet famously learned how to overcome these handicaps, communicate with the world, and spread her lectures promoting optimism. An inspiring read for everyone... Biographies/Inspirational Pages 84

Sara Crewe *by Frances Burnett*   ISBN: *1-59462-360-0*   **$9.45**

In the first place, Miss Minchin lived in London. Her home was a large, dull, tall one, in a large, dull square, where all the houses were alike, and all the sparrows were alike, and where all the door-knockers made the same heavy sound... Childrens/Classic Pages 88

The Autobiography of Benjamin Franklin *by Benjamin Franklin*   ISBN: *1-59462-135-7*   **$24.95**

The Autobiography of Benjamin Franklin has probably been more extensively read than any other American historical work, and no other book of its kind has had such ups and downs of fortune. Franklin lived for many years in England, where he was agent... Biographies/History Pages 332

Name	
Email	
Telephone	
Address	
City, State ZIP	

☐ Credit Card   ☐ Check / Money Order

Credit Card Number	
Expiration Date	
Signature	

Please Mail to: Book Jungle
                     PO Box 2226
                     Champaign, IL 61825
or Fax to: 630-214-0564

ORDERING INFORMATION

web*: www.bookjungle.com*
email*: sales@bookjungle.com*
fax*: 630-214-0564*
mail*: Book Jungle PO Box 2226 Champaign, IL 61825*
or PayPal *to sales@bookjungle.com*

Please contact us for bulk discounts

DIRECT-ORDER TERMS

**20% Discount if You Order
Two or More Books**
Free Domestic Shipping!
Accepted: Master Card, Visa,
Discover, American Express

www.ingramcontent.com/pod-product-compliance
Lightning Source LLC
Chambersburg PA
CBHW080700110426
42739CB00034B/3352